MARATHON TRAINING STRATEGIES

MARATHON TRAINING STRATEGIES

A COMPREHENSIVE GUIDE TO RUNNING YOUR BEST MARATHON - INCLUDING PLANS, ADVICE, AND GOAL-HITTING TIPS

JOHN MCDONNELL

GREATIVE
BOOKS PUBLISHING, LTD

DEDICATION

This book has been made possible by all the amazing runners, coaches, clubs and volunteers I've met, or been a part of, throughout the years. There are so many individuals, but to name a single runner who has been the most positive influence in my enjoyment and progression in the sport, I dedicate this book to Tara Malone. We have been on a similar trajectory for a long time and it has been a pleasure and an honour to witness all your success and to share your joy of running.

ABOUT THE AUTHOR

John McDonnell is a UK Athletics Coach in Running Fitness. He has written several books on running as well as his memoir describing how the sport of running saved his life.

At the age of 48, he was a healthy and fit marathon runner who was progressing in the sport on a personal level and had been coaching other runners for three years. Then, out of the blue, he suffered a stroke. It turned out to be caused by an 11mm hole in his heart. He had heart surgery, called an ASD closure, later that same year. It was however, the sport of running that ensured he was strong enough to return to life, relatively close to the same as he was before the stroke.

It was the coaching of other runners that kept his sanity during the months of rehab and no racing. Needless to say, running has defined John for many years now and continues to do so today. He has built his brand around A Heart for Running and you can view his personal and coaching content by clicking the links below.

He also hosts much of his coaching content on Achieve Running Club social media accounts. The Achieve Running

Club is a free support network of runners for runners. Please reach out at any of his social media outlets as John is keen to help runners achieve their running goals, whatever they may be.

- facebook.com/aheartforrunning
- instagram.com/aheart4running
- amazon.com/author/aheartforrunning
- tiktok.com/@aheartforrunning

DISCLAIMER

Keeping physically active is key to maintaining a healthy lifestyle. But it is always best to check with your doctor before taking part in any sport, like running, to ensure it is safe for you to do so. Although this is geared to experienced runners, please ensure you get clearance from your doctor as the intensity of some of these programs are quite high.

COPYRIGHT

First published in 2022 by Greative Books Publishing, Ltd.
Grogey Road
Fivemiletown
Tyrone
BT75 0NT

Copyright © John McDonnell, 2023

The moral right of the author has been asserted

Every effort has been made to trace copyright holders and to obtain their permission for the use of copyrighted material. The publisher apologises for any errors or omissions and would be grateful if notified of any corrections that should be incorporated in future reprints of this book.

All rights reserved. No part of this publication may be reproduced, stored in a retrieval system, or transmitted in any form or by any means, electronic, mechanical, photocopying, recording or otherwise, without the prior written permission from the publishers.

Book Cover Design: Owen McDonnell & Thea Chetcuti

ISBN Paperback: 978-1-7395471-0-3
ISBN Ebook: 978-1-7395471-1-0

CONTENTS

HOW TO USE THIS BOOK	1
Introduction	3
YOUR TRAINING PLAN & TRAINING LOG	14
A Plan	14
A Training Log	17
Key Metrics	18
Training Notes	19
RUNNING SHOES & GEAR	22
Running Shoes	22
The Rest of Your Running Gear	26
PHYSICAL PREPARATION	29
Physical Preparation	29
Cross Training	29
Sleep	32
STRETCHING & SELF MAINTENANCE	34
Stretching and Self Maintenance	34
Yoga	35
Sports Massage	36
Foam Rolling	38
Rest Days	38
NUTRITION & HYDRATION	39
Nutrition & Hydration	39
Carbohydrates	40
Protein	41
Fats	42

Hydration	43
Electrolytes	45
Preparing Nutritionally for Race Day	46
Gels & In Race Nutrition	48
Caffeine	50
Alcohol	50
BUILDING A POSITIVE MINDSET	52
Positive Mindset	52
Visualization	52
Affirmations	55
Positive Self-Talk	56
Mental Techniques - Counting Your Cadence	58
Mental Techniques - Using a Breathing Pattern	59
RACE WEIGHT	60
Race Weight	60
The Stillman Calculation	60
The Stillman Calculation for Women	61
The Stillman Calculation for Men	61
The Stillman Calculation for Long Distance Athletes	62
How and When to Lose Weight	64
When to Gain Weight	66
A Brief Discussion on BMR (Basal Metabolic Rate)	66
FURTHER ADVICE LEADING TO RACE DAY	68
Tapering	68
Preparing for All Weather Conditions	70
Race Day Plans (Plan A, Plan B and Plan C)	72
Running with a Pacer	72
Determining Whether You Are On Target	73
Advice and Tips for the Week Before Race Day	74

Rest	74
Sleep	75
Body Preparations	75
Evening Before Race Day	76
Pre-Race Evening Meal	77
Preparing your Race Bag for the Bag Drop	78
YOUR MARATHON DAY & BEYOND	80
Advice and Tips for Race Day	80
Wake Up	80
Breakfast	81
Arriving at the Start Line	82
First Mile	83
Second Mile	84
Miles Three through Twelve	85
Half-Way Point	85
20 Miles	86
24 Miles	86
Last Mile	87
Post Marathon	89
Evening	89
First Two Weeks After Your Marathon	90
Three Weeks Out	90
Pick Your Next Marathon Target	91
THE PLANS	92
Guide to Different Session Paces	93
Effectively Executing the Long Slow Distance Run	96
A Brief Note About Running by Feel	99
Digital Plan Templates	100
PERSONAL COACHING	101

Sub 4:00 Plan - Medium Mileage Plan	103
Sub 3:45 Plan - Medium Mileage Plan	121
Sub 3:30 Plan - Medium Mileage Plan	139
Sub 3:15 Plan - Medium Mileage Plan	159
Sub 3:00 Plan - High Mileage Plan	179
Sub 2:45 Plan - High Mileage Plan	197
Afterword	215
Also by John McDonnell	217

HOW TO USE THIS BOOK

THERE ARE six marathon training plans at the back of this book. However, the content of the book is just as important as any plan in helping you achieve your goal. Make sure to read, understand and incorporate as many of these techniques before beginning any of the plans.

The training strategies I discuss are the keys to hitting your targets. The plans are the vehicle you will use to get you there. But the vehicle is of no use without the keys. The strategies and the 16-week training plans work together to build an athlete up, both physically and mentally, to be prepared to tackle the challenge ahead.

Some of these strategies will seem strange to veteran runners. Don't let that stop you from trying them out. One 16-week training block is all it will take to make you a believer in the advice I'm giving. These are proven techniques and it's time the sport of running incorporated these into our training.

Most importantly, enjoy the process. Take note of the changes in your body; in your running form; in your mental strength. Be proud of your progress. By following this advice you will be amazed at your results. Now go forth and conquer your marathon goals.

INTRODUCTION

I started running as a method to lose weight. I was 50 lbs too heavy and looked every bit of it. I had a young family and I knew I needed to do something for myself to improve my fitness, if not for me, at least for them. I began slowly, and it definitely wasn't easy. It was ages before I was able to complete a mile without stopping. Eventually, with perseverance, or some may say bull-headedness, I started to see progress. Weight was falling off and I was able to run further distances, maybe not fast, but for longer. Soon after completing my first 5k, I moved up to a 10k. The progression continued until out of the blue I decided it was time for a marathon. The prospect intrigued me, and I embraced it. With very little knowledge about the sport, I turned my attention to running more often and longer weekend runs. Then, in early 2013 I did it. I ran my first marathon.

There is something magical about being able to say that. Over the course of 4 hours and 22 minutes I went from being a runner to being a marathoner. That is a title that nobody would ever be able to take away from me. It was a badge I wore with pride and still do to this day. That day, more than most, put me on my trajectory to becoming a running coach and a marathon enthusiast. I've completed over 35 official marathons and countless more in training. There is something about those hours on my feet that I find therapeutic, comforting in a strange, twisted sort of way.

When it comes to marathon racing, that's a different ball game. That's when the blinkers go on and tunnel vision kicks in. I find myself laser focussed on the race and thinking about all the different aspects that I need to do. Planning the next water stop and the next gel to make sure I can hold my pace. Calculating the miles and minutes in my head over and over determining if I'm on target for my goal. Recalling all the successful training sessions over the previous 16 weeks. I feel the pain, but with solid preparation, I'm able to stay positive, push through, and maintain my pace. The miles build up behind me and I'm seeing the latter sections of the race as I did in my mind for so long. Turning this corner and the next one, pushing on until I see the finish line. I know I will hit my goal. This is the buzz of marathon racing. This is what all the hard work is all about. My physical and mental well-being thrives in this environment. As we all know, it is about "embracing the suck."

When it comes to marathon racing, the opinions and available advice vary greatly as to how to achieve your best performance on race day. To be honest, most coaches will follow a similar philosophy and we all understand the concepts of load, rest, and adaptation. The key differences seem to be how much load and how much rest. I use my own BPR periodization system. BPR is Base, Pace, Race and is slightly different from a lot of other coaches, but it has proven to be a highly successful method for myself and my athletes. We will build strength and stamina in the Base phase. In the Pace phase we will build up speed endurance and this is the longest phase of the plan. Finally, we have the Race phase where we will taper, remain sharp, and prepare for race day. Depending on the athlete's current level, the length of each phase can be different, but the concepts remain. I also adhere to best practices for my athletes and their injury prevention. the ultimate goal is to arrive at the start line on race day in tip-top condition, peaking at just the right time.

What I offer here is advice to people who have struggled to reach their goals in a marathon race. My personal progression and that of my athlete's will speak for itself. Whether trying to break four hours or three, you will find information here that you may not have thought of before and will certainly help you finally achieve that elusive personal record (PR), or personal best (PB), depending on where you are from.

There are six marathon training plans included in the

back of this book. They range from a sub-four hour finish all the way down to a 2:45 finish, and every 15 minutes in between. Pick the one that is right for you. Be realistic, practical and commit to it. Once you've committed to taking this on, and you follow the advice in this book, nothing can stop you.

My plans aren't just about running however. You will find advice here that has helped me personally not only become a better runner, but a more well rounded individual, boosting confidence and my quality of life. This has translated to the running circuit with huge success. Outside of the running plans, the physical and mental preparation work have the potential to transform your life for the better. 16 weeks of hard work and commitment. You know you can do it.

This process will require trust. Trust in the methods I'm deploying for you and trust in your own ability. There is a big difference between *running* a marathon and *racing* a marathon. I cover how to race, from mile 1 to mile 26.2. These are tried and tested methods. Professional sports personalities have been using them for decades. Not all of them are well-known in the running world, but the best of the best are using them. There will be nothing left on the table, you will receive all of the tips and pointers that will get you to your marathon running goals.

So why should you trust me? I've been running marathons since 2013, when I ran my first one as a complete novice. My progression as a marathon runner is documented below in Table A. It speaks for itself as far as the training techniques and methods go.

I've now coached over a thousand runners from nearly every background and ability. This number includes countless individual marathoners. There is nothing more satisfying for a coach than to see their athletes hit their goals and achieve things they never thought possible. That's what brings me such joy and satisfaction.

Personal Marathon Running Progression

Year	Marathon	Finishing Time
2013	Sximilebridge (my first marathon)	4:22:58
2013	Cork City Marathon	3:49:57
2014	Longford Marathon (My first BQ)	3:24:33
2015	Newry City Marathon	3:19:09
2016	Dublin City Marathon	3:14:23
2017	*Dublin City Marathon	3:43:22
2018	Exeter Marathon	3:15:53
2019	Chester Marathon	3:06:07
2020	No marathons due to Covid restrictions, however I completed the Donadea 50k in 3:50:50 to win the Irish Over 50 50k national championship	------
2021	Out for the year with an injury	------
2022	Kildare Thoroughbred Marathon	2:58:44
2023	TCS London Marathon	2:56:33

Table A. My Personal Marathon Progression

*In February 2017 I suffered a stroke and later underwent heart surgery in November. I was extremely fortunate that the event occurred in the manner it did. You can read my entire story in the book *A Heart for Running*.

My progression has been helped along over the years by the data I've collected about my own running. Keeping detailed logs, studying what works for me and what doesn't.

Understanding my body and when and how it runs best. There has been an awful lot of learning as well from other coaches and athletes. This will be a learning experience for you as well, about yourself and your body. You should keep detailed notes of all you do, and the things you learn here, so that you can use it going forward in future events.

What is so special about marathon running? This, ultimately, is the question underlying our sport. Why do it? Why is it special? What does it mean to me (you)? This may not be your first marathon and you should know how hard it is to run a competitive marathon time. Competitive is a relative term and rightfully so. A competitive marathon time for you might be 3:59:59, while for others it may be 2:29:59. But you want to take that next step and make an improvement on your personal record.

You'll be introduced to tips and advice that so many first-timers never even considered. When I ran my first marathon, I was a complete novice. I knew nothing, other than I was fairly confident that I could complete the distance. I knew this because I had nearly done so in training. If I had all of this information provided in this book earlier in my running life, I may have broken the 3-hour barrier much earlier. Instead, it took over 30 marathons before achieving this milestone.

Still, I don't think I would have changed a thing about my progression. I learned so much about the sport, and more importantly about myself. I made hundreds of friends and covered thousands of miles. I visited so many interesting places and ran so many iconic races. These marathons have defined my running life. It is a distance that is dear to my heart.

I think marathon running is so special because it is hard. I suppose any running is hard, but 26.2 miles of pushing yourself to your limit takes it to another level. Let's face it, in order to run your best race, you have to push to the edge of your limits the whole way. This is why there is such a feeling of achievement when it is done. It can also be such an emotional experience for a great many people. Marathon running takes such commitment and strength over such a long time that it is an accomplishment just making it to the start line in one piece. That is also why when things don't go to plan it can feel emotionally devastating. To spend 16 weeks, or more, training hard, hitting your session targets, cross training, eating right, basically doing all the right things, and to still miss out on your goal it can be demoralizing. The most important thing to remember in this case is to take something away from the experience. What went wrong? What could you do differently? There is a learning opportunity from every run, be it a race or a training run.

Nobody would challenge their bodies in this way if they didn't like the pain, or at least appreciate the hard effort. Why else would you do it, time and again? That's the thing, very few people do one marathon and stop there. Despite what our brain tells us during our races, we always look towards the next one within a few days of finishing one. There is something a little sadistic about a marathon runner. We cherish the aches and pains we feel every morning getting out of bed. We know we are training and running well because it is sore to walk. Our bodies creak and moan at every step, until it is time to run. It is then that our sore hamstrings and aching ankles loosen up and we can stride out after the first mile and start to feel the wind in our face. We feel the beautiful motion of our arms driving our legs forward. The aches melt away, mile after mile.

Our brains are talking to us the whole time we are running. We are figuring out a problem at work or at home. We get lost in our thoughts. We solve our problems. We get inspiring and creative ideas. It is an hour or two of blissful escapism. After finishing our run, we get a short stretch done and head for home. When it comes to successful marathoning, everything has a purpose. What we do before our run. How we execute the training session for the day. How we stretch after the run. How we re-fuel our bodies with food, nutrients and water. How well we sleep. If you are to run your best marathon, and want to ensure you hit your target, everything is planned. Living deliberately like this has so many other positive side effects, running a great race is just one of them.

In order to pull off this feat, you have to be willing to put in an unusually hard effort and a grueling amount of work. In today's society, everyone is looking for the easy way out. How to run a marathon with the least effort. If that is your mindset, this book probably isn't for you. However, I am guessing that you are reading this book because you know what the benefits of all this hard work will be. You know that the feeling of satisfaction you will have after achieving your goal will be well worth the effort. You know that nobody will ever be able to take the accomplishment away from you. You know that all those who doubted you will have to show you a little more respect for your commitment and passion for self-improvement.

Or maybe you come from the opposite perspective. Maybe you've done everything you thought you could do and had disappointing results. You know you could and should do better. You may need to figure out what more you can do to get to that next level. This is what we aim for here. Next level marathon results.

There is a special feeling when you train hard, for 16 weeks, and arrive at the start line of a marathon, big or small, in one piece. By this time, you have done the work, you've not made any silly mistakes leading up to the race start. You can visualize the clock as you cross the finish line, and it is ticking just under your goal time. Everything has fallen into place. This is the perfect situation. Now, it very seldom works out *exactly* to plan, but there is a lot within your powers to put yourself into position to make it come as close as possible and sometimes even better.

What we can do is take control of the things within our

sphere of influence. We can do the training, stretch, eat right, strength train, take rest days, sleep, and so much more. I will go over all of these points throughout the course of this book in much more detail, however, there is always one underlying question, "how bad do you want it?" Or more importantly, I like to ask, "what are you willing to do to make it happen?" Those athlete's who can answer, "whatever it takes!" and mean it will be successful.

It's no wonder that after a really good marathon race many of us just want to run off-plan for a while. Just run without the discipline and focus. Being able to enjoy the company on a group run without paying attention to the pace is liberating. However, it doesn't take long before we are ready to get back to the routine; the regiment of following a plan. It gives structure to our running once again. There is something equally as *liberating* in a weird and twisted sense of the word.

In this book, I will discuss all aspects of what it will take to run your best marathon. There is a saying that goes, "your fastest marathon will be your easiest." There is a perfectly logical reason for this. It is because it will be the marathon for which you are best prepared. You did the work. You committed to the program. You prepared both physically and mentally. You didn't take the easy way out. Imagine that feeling when the work is done, the race is run, and you are in the finishers' funnel beaming with pride with a shiny new personal record. That is why it is all worth it.

It is a special challenge for each of you and I'm here to tell you that you can reach your realistic goals. You can do remarkable things. Your body is capable of incredible feats of endurance. Trust yourself, trust your training and trust your coach, who has been there and proved it can be done. Good luck.

YOUR TRAINING PLAN & TRAINING LOG

SO WHAT IS it going to take? There are several factors that will be involved. I include six targeted plans at the back of this book. You need to choose the right one for you. Be realistic and practical, but also go in with optimism and self-belief. Know that with hard work and commitment can come a remarkable transformation.

A PLAN

I've developed endless plans for my athletes over the years. I know that runners and particularly marathon runners need a plan to follow, or at least specific weekly direction in order to get into race day shape come the end of the training block. A good plan will cover a number of different bases for the athlete. First, and most importantly, a good plan will give the runner the sessions required to cause the appropriate adaptation enabling them to hit their target. This needs to be realistic and achievable.

The plan should be broken down into the correct periodized phases of the appropriate length to make the best use of the adaptation that has taken place from the previous phase. In other words, going from building the base, to working on pace, to preparing for the race (BPR), with each phase transitioning at the correct point. This sounds way more complex than it is in reality. But there is a method to the different phases and these should be adhered to.

The plan needs to give the best sessions to the athlete that will stack up with injury prevention in mind. Giving too many hard sessions consecutively will not only have a negative adaptation effect, but is a formula almost guaranteeing an injury. It should avoid too many high load weeks back to back as well. The human body changes to the stress it is put under, but too much stress will cause a breakdown somewhere. The right plan for the individual will ensure that over-training is avoided.

Every coach has their own way of training their athletes. Over the years, I've developed my own three phase method of marathon training. My BPR method is not revolutionary, but it simplifies the process and makes planning both straightforward and highly successful.

Phase I: Building the **Base**

In this phase the focus is to start building the miles,

working on strength, stability, balance, coordination. During this first 3-7 week period, the length depends on many factors, my athletes will have very little speed work. However, there will be hills, hilly runs, a slow build up in both the weekly long run as well as the weekly overall mileage. There will certainly be training runs with differing paces, however, it will focus on relative pace, not necessarily race specific pace. This means there will be more easy, steady and long slow distance runs relative to any speed sessions. Speaking in generalities, the faster the target time, the shorter the base phase is.

Phase II: Training for **Pace**

Training for pace is where things start to get a little more targeted. This phase can last between 6 to 11 weeks. While we continue to work on strength, stability, balance and coordination, we now start to progressively work on pace. There are more weekly speed and speed endurance sessions. The focus is more to train athletes to hold the race pace for the full 26.2 miles and finish strong. The types of sessions included in this phase will be intervals, progressions, tempo runs, race-pace runs, as well as easy, steady and long slow distance runs.

It is important to remember than in this phase, particularly towards the end of it, your body will be tired. Because of all the hard training, it will be more difficult to hit target paces on certain runs. This should not be discouraging. This should prove that the plan is working. Ultimately, you should be able to hit most of the targets, but it is only after your taper will you be in peak condition.

Phase III: Final Preparation for the **Race**

Final race specific sessions, with race targets in mind, along with a taper, make up this final Race phase. This is the last 2 to 3 weeks of the 16 week plan. The length of the Race phase depends greatly on the athlete, their specific goal as well as how the training has been going. The idea here is to make the most of the practical adaptation before the training effect is wasted. In other words, not to push the runner to fatigue too close to race day. We are aiming to arrive at the start line feeling fresh, strong and like a coiled spring, ready to attack the race. It is at the end of this Race phase where you should peak physically on race day.

One of the other important aspects of this phase is reinforcing the positive mental outlook going into the race. This is where positive self-talk, visualization and other mental techniques will come to play a bigger part. Whether the Race Phase is 3 weeks or 10 days, we will build and strengthen our mind game. The goal is to be feeling so prepared for the race that nothing can get in the way of success.

A TRAINING LOG

You have your plan, now you need a method to log your training sessions. The main objective for logging each of your training sessions is that you can see what is working and what is not working. To see progress or lack thereof. The ability to go back and interrogate the data and make changes for your next training block based on actual relevant information. There are countless possibilities for doing this and any number of details of which to keep track. There are apps and traditional paper log books for a start. Quite a few runners will tell you that they use their GPS sports watch for this task. For reasons I'll explain below, I don't think this is the best method for logging. I prefer to use a fairly complex spreadsheet that I created and keep meticulous notes of different key metrics as well as session notes.

KEY METRICS

Among the key metrics I choose to log include the following:

- A weekly weigh-in done on the same day of the week each week
- Daily water consumption (and daily average for the week)
- Daily calorie consumption (and daily average for the week)
- This is further broken down by macro (protein, carbohydrate, fat)
- Daily average resting heart rate (and daily average for the week)
- Weekly running mileage

- Nightly hours of sleep (and nightly average for the week)
- How many daily minutes of strength training (and total for the week)
- How many daily minutes of yoga/stretching (and total for the week)

The benefit of having all of this data is that there is a complete story being told. When combined with my daily training notes, it gives me a fully comprehensive picture of how my training is going. When looking back on how I prepared for a race, I can see precisely what went well, and what didn't and it will inform my next training block. If it can be measured, it can be improved.

TRAINING NOTES

When logging my daily training notes, even when it is a rest day, I am very specific. So if it was a running session I will include:

- How many miles I covered
- What type of run it was
- What trainers I wore
- What average pace I ran at
- If it was an interval session or a session with target paces per mile, I will break down the pace

for each rep and/or mile. As an example, a 10 mile progression would be logged showing the pace for each mile
- Who I ran with
- What the weather was like
- Where I ran
- How I felt before, during, and after the run
- Any niggles or soreness
- If I had a sports massage or any other self-care treatment
- Any other bit of information that may prove interesting

Personally, I log all of this information every morning by collating the data from different apps as logged the day before. I know you will find most of this data on these apps, like Strava or Garmin Connect, however, pulling it all together into one spreadsheet makes much more of an impact. You will see the entire story in one place, without having to review each session in your different apps which is incredibly time consuming. So time consuming in fact, that I doubt anyone actually does it. This spreadsheet will make for very interesting reading months and years after your target race, I can promise you that. It will also help you plan your future races in a much more thoughtful and relevant manner.

I have spent the last few years refining my training log template that I use for my own training. These have been made available on the Achieve Running Club website. The Google Sheets, or the alternative Excel Spreadsheets, for each of the plans in this book, are available at an 80% discount for purchaser's of this book. You can find these templates at https://achieverc.com/marathon-plan-templates/. Just use Discount Code: **MTS_BPD** on checkout to receive your price reduction.

RUNNING SHOES & GEAR

RUNNING SHOES

IF YOU ARE READING this book in order to run your fastest marathon, then you probably have a good idea what kind of running shoes suit you best by now. You've probably run a marathon or two already, which hopefully, you prepared for, and are used to running fairly heavy miles during the course of your training. When selecting the right shoe for you, it is best to experiment. Yes, gait analysis is useful, but I find that there is no substitute for running in the actual shoes and seeing how they feel. Over time, you should get to know the particular characteristics you should be looking out for when choosing the right type of shoes.

The running shoes should be the first thing you get right in your preparation. These will be hitting the ground roughly between 35,000 and 45,000 times during the course of the 26.2 mile race. There are simply too many chances to experience discomfort. Over the course of the first 4 weeks, you should know what shoes work best for you, for both training and for race day. They may very well be different. If you are wearing a different shoe on race day than you train in, then make sure you put your race-day shoes on for a few short, fast sessions and at least one medium/long run well before race day. You'll ideally have at least 30 miles done in them before your event.

When breaking in the racing shoes, the reason I suggest using them on the faster sessions is because you want these to *feel* like your racing shoes. You should feel fast when these are on your feet. They should feel special, significant, and different from ordinary trainers. They still need to be broken in, but by doing it on the shorter, faster sessions, you'll know they are your fast shoes. When race day comes around and you slip on your racers your brain knows it's time to run fast, you have a better chance of doing just that.

Although not necessary, there are several benefits to regularly rotating training shoes over the course of a 16-week training cycle. These include a reduced risk of injury, improved performance, not to mention the longevity of your investment in running shoes. The idea is to alternate between multiple pairs during training, even different brands. Each pair of shoes will provide a different type of support and cushioning, which can help prevent repetitive strain and overuse injuries. When training in the same shoes, repeatedly, your feet and legs are subjected to the same stresses and strains over and over again. This can lead to shin splints, stress fractures and plantar fasciitis. By rotating between your different running shoes, you distribute the impact and pressure more evenly. It also can have a positive effect on your running mechanics. A rotation almost forces you to maintain focus on good running form which in turn improves your speed, endurance and running economy.

As for getting the most from your investment in your shoes, a good rotation of at least three pairs will go a long way toward keeping them in decent shape. Rather than wearing them out quickly, by swapping them daily, weekly or as you change your running surface, you are keeping each pair fresher for longer and getting the benefit of the latest shoe technology for the duration of your training cycle.

In order to have a rotation, start with at least two pairs of shoes for training and one pair that you will race in. Each pair will probably have differing levels of support and cushioning, and maybe be different brands. Perhaps the pair with the best cushioning are used for the longer runs while others are used for shorter runs. More than three pairs is useful as well, but we aren't all made of money. Considering the cost of today's running shoes, it may not be practical to have more than three. Two might even be a push, but if it's feasible, it is a good idea.

The earlier in your 16 week cycle that the rotation is

decided, the better. As you make your way through your training weeks, pay close attention to the wear patterns on the soles. If one pair is wearing out faster than the others, you may need to retire them or adjust your rotation to use them less frequently. Additionally, when working with a new pair of shoes, listen closely to your body. This is essential and if you experience any prolonged discomfort in a pair of shoes, remove them from your rotation immediately. Take note as to the discomfort and when it started. Check back in your training log as to when you put a new pair of trainers into your rotation and see if there is a connection.

Running shoes utilizing the latest technology really do make a difference. I don't think it's easily quantifiable as to how much of a difference, but there's no doubt that records have been falling since the introduction of the Nike ZoomX foam and the carbon plated trainers. Other brands have followed suit with advancements of their own. I've heard some crazy figures thrown around as to how much the new tech will take off every runner's race times, as high as 15 seconds per mile. I don't agree that it is that significant, but there is something there.

Besides providing more bounce for the distance runner, the newer technology provides a more cushioned experience. With the right running shoe, you may find that your feet don't hurt in the latter miles of a marathon the way they would have years ago. I recommend you try the latest brands and you choose the most advanced shoe you can reasonably afford.

As for the argument over whether we should be wearing the new technically advanced shoes or not, it's a no brainer for me. Technology has been improving in the world of running for decades. Nobody can say that the runners who broke the world records in the 80's and 90's didn't have technically far better shoes than what they wore in the 60's and 70's. Advancements are made all the time and to say we can't take advantage of them is just wrong. Fast trainers will not make a slow runner fast. Nor will slow trainers make a fast runner slow. The technology certainly helps, but take advantage of it and be grateful to have better shoes than your parents did.

THE REST OF YOUR RUNNING GEAR

There is a reason this is called "The Rest of *Your* Running Gear." Everybody is different. We all perform best when our own needs are met. The running shoes I find best, might cause considerable pain for you. The cut of one pair of shorts might not fit the same on someone else. The singlet I like, may rub uncomfortably under your arms. Suffice it to say, like most things when it comes to running, you'll need to experiment. The most important thing is to experiment well before race day.

A brief story to highlight this point. A number of years

ago, I signed up to do a local half marathon. I needed new shorts, so I ordered them online and they arrived the day before the race. What could go wrong with a new pair of shorts, right? They looked fine, they fit fine, seriously, what could go wrong? I wore them on race day, which happened to be a wet, miserable day to start. All was going fine, until around mile 5 when my inner thighs began to chafe. Before long, it was getting unbearable. By mile 8, I was running like I was John Wayne entering a saloon. I had to make a point to try to keep my legs further apart. Needless to say, the shower after this particular race was excruciating. After a few days, my thighs scabbed over and it was ok, but that taught me a lesson I'll never forget. Test everything before race day.

We all know that we need to test out new running shoes and the same goes for every bit of gear. Socks, underwear, singlets, shorts, gel-belts, gloves, hats, even sunglasses. Anything and everything. Wouldn't it be a shame to train hard for 16 weeks, arrive at the start line healthy and in great shape for your target marathon, only to fall short of your goal because you didn't test something you are wearing. Yet, it happens over and over again to runners of all experience levels. We all face this at one point or another, but if you can learn from other people's mistakes, then please do.

For your clothing, make sure everything has been worn a few times before marathon day. They should have been worn and washed at least twice before you decide to wear them on the one day that counts. Different materials will chafe your skin when they are brand new and often only soften after a couple of washes. You seriously need to do these little things to give yourself the best chance to do well. Why wouldn't you? They don't take much effort; just a bit of planning in the weeks ahead of showtime.

There is one last thing to point out about race day running gear. That is to make sure that you wear something that makes you feel good. Much like going on a job interview, where you are advised to dress in such a way to make you feel most confident. When we look good, we feel good. We feel confident and empowered. The same goes for what you wear on race day. Wear a pair of shorts or leggings that boost your confidence because you look and feel good in them. Your appearance can give you a genuine increase in your performance. This is all part of your mental preparation which goes hand-in-hand with your physical preparation.

PHYSICAL PREPARATION

PHYSICAL PREPARATION

WHAT IS physical preparation in marathon training? Well, it is a broad brush term that basically takes into account all the work that goes into getting your body physically ready for running your best marathon. For us, it consists of aerobic conditioning, strength training, flexibility and mobility training, nutrition and rest. Each of these things come into play when it comes to reaching your target race in the best possible condition.

CROSS TRAINING

Because the marathon is a long-distance race, it requires you to build up your endurance through regular cardiovascular exercise. We do a lot of cardio in the way of our running training already. However, it is best practice to also cross train with other exercises like cycling, swimming, and/or aerobic classes. The possibilities are endless. Doing some exercise that gets your heart rate up for an extended period of time will help build your aerobic capacity. Running should make up the vast majority of the time spent on cardio, but for injury prevention, cross training is beneficial.

Swimming and cycling seem to be the two favorite methods of cross-training for many runners. The obvious reason is that both of these are less impactful than running and, therefore, can be done often without taking a negative toll on the running sessions. These are excellent and well worth considering as a source of cross-training.

In addition to aerobic conditioning, strength training is a massive benefit to endurance runners. I would go so far as to say essential. A good strong core as well as lower body strength will improve speed, endurance and allow you to finish the race strong. One of the reasons that this is the case might not seem so obvious. As you are training and the miles are piling up, you will most likely be losing a few pounds of body weight. What you don't want to lose is muscle mass. Ideally, any weight loss should come in the form of fat loss. Maintaining existing muscle and building stronger muscle fibers is extremely important. But remember, you are an endurance runner, not a bodybuilder. Be sure to consume sufficient nutrition to stay strong, just not too much where you bulk up. We are aiming for light, lean and strong.

A good strong core will also aid in two other aspects of running that often get overlooked. Balance and coordination are neglected areas for many runners, but working on these two things are also beneficial. Think about it. By definition, running requires a person to only have at most one foot on the ground at any one time. Your body will subconsciously auto-adjust any balance issues with each stride. Therefore, if you can give your body the least amount of extra work during the course of a 26.2 mile run, the better it will perform. Coordination offers similar benefits. Both good balance and good coordination make maintaining good running form much easier to maintain over the distance. Solid running mechanics will ensure you cover the distance in the most efficient manner possible.

Strength Training Routine

A good routine that I recommend is to perform a 20 minute bodyweight circuit every morning, or at least five days per week. The circuit consists of the following exercises:

- Push-ups
- Crunches
- Plank
- Squats
- Dead Bugs
- Bicycle Crunches
- Lunges

Do these in sets of 10, 20, 30, etc….and keep repeating until you reach a total of 20 minutes. Perform 50 of each and do 2 sets and it takes 20 minutes. If sets of 50 are too hard to begin with, perform sets of 20, you may have to run through the circuit three or four times, or sets of 10 five times. For the plank, try to work up to a 2 minute plank each time, but start wherever you are at now.

SLEEP

Adaptation is the process that occurs in the body as a result of consistent training. These changes include improvements in cardiovascular function, muscle strength and endurance. Adaptation typically occurs over a period of several weeks to months of consistent training and exercise. During this time, the body undergoes a series of changes in response to the demands your running training places upon it.

Sleep plays an important role in the adaptation process for runners. During sleep, the body undergoes a variety of physiological processes that are essential for physical recovery from exercise. One important process that occurs during sleep is the release of growth hormone, which is essential for tissue repair and recovery. Sleep also plays a crucial role in the regulation of the immune system, hormone production and metabolism. Each of these is important for overall health and athletic performance.

Studies have shown that sleep deprivation can have a negative impact on athletic performance and recovery. On the other hand, getting enough high-quality sleep will improve athletic performance, reduce the risk of injury and promote a healthy lifestyle, both physically and mentally.

Throughout your 16-week training program, you should be aiming to get as much good quality sleep as possible. You should be prioritizing sleep over nights out, late night tv, and other activities that keep you from your bed. We all require different amounts of sleep to perform at our best, and you know your own body better than anyone. For most of us, this will mean between seven and nine hours of sleep per night. The best science at the minute suggests that we follow both a bedtime routine as well as a morning routine. The most basic concept is to try to get up at the same time every morning and follow some sort of routine. This is the case no matter what time you get to bed in the evening.

This concept will probably not work if you do shift-work or cannot follow a routine for one reason or another. In such a case, just ensure you prioritize sleep over any other activity when you should be sleeping.

For an evening routine, it is recommended that we switch off electronics a good hour before bed. That includes the tv, computers, video games, and phones. Then about 30 minutes before bed find a nice quiet place to sit in peace and quiet. Eventually, shut the lights out about 10 minutes before going to bed. Then when you are feeling drowsy, head into bed and sleep well for the night.

STRETCHING & SELF MAINTENANCE

STRETCHING AND SELF MAINTENANCE

MOST OF THE runners I know tend to be somewhat *relaxed* about dynamic warmups and post run stretching. However, those that do partake of these important running routines are less likely to experience injuries. It's not a guarantee of injury prevention, and it could possibly be correlation as opposed to causation, but why take that chance. A few minutes to warm up and a few minutes of stretching certainly isn't going to cause an injury.

There are also some very useful tools in the runners repertoire that will also help greatly. Yoga, sports massage, foam rolling all have a place in the marathon runners' training regime.

YOGA

I'm not a yoga instructor. Nor do I pretend that I'm particularly good at it. However, I do know the benefits are amazing for runners. A few yoga workouts of 30-60 minutes every week will go a long way over the course of a 16 week training cycle. It is hard to say if it is the key to injury prevention or not, however, I do believe it can play a big part.

Yoga is a fantastic form of exercise for runners. It combines manoeuvring into different poses that involve building strength, breathing exercises and meditation. When doing yoga on a regular basis there are numerous health benefits such as reducing stress, improving flexibility and runners will find an increase in strength and balance. It can help improve performance and reduce the risk of injury and promote faster recovery.

There are literally thousands of videos online with different routines and demonstrations of how to do each pose. Some routines are specifically put together for runners. These yoga sessions are particularly effective the morning after a long run, or an intense speed session. However, there is no bad time to practice yoga. If there is a yoga studio nearby, I suggest going to a live instructor and explain that you are preparing for a marathon. Discuss with them the areas where you are feeling tightness or strain and ask if they can include a few poses that will address these areas. There is no harm in asking and a good yoga instructor will not mind tailoring a small part of their routine for the needs of their clients.

SPORTS MASSAGE

Have you ever told someone you were going for a sports massage and they replied that it sounds nice and relaxing? That person has never had a sports massage. A good deep tissue sports massage can be painful, especially if it's been a long time between sessions. However, a day or two after having one, you may very well feel like a new person. It's kind of like an oil change in a car. One good sports massage and you're good to run for another four weeks, pain free. So why is that?

The vast majority of us who run marathons do so as recreation. We don't have the luxury of doing it as a full-time occupation. Therefore, we have our daily commutes to work where we are in the car for a period of time. Perhaps we find ourselves sitting at a desk for 6-8 hours a day. This conditions the body to keep muscles in a shortened state. In order to keep our muscles in the most effective condition, we need to keep them lengthened and flexible.

As runners we tend to use the same muscles, over and over. Our posterior chain, for example, consists of three groups of muscles in the back lower half of the body; the calves, hamstrings, and glutes. There are also three in the upper body, rear shoulders, lats and the muscles along both sides of the spine. As your body propels you forward, during a run, it is contracting these muscles over and over, particularly the lower half of the chain, but to some extent the upper body as well. This, in turn, causes them to shorten, as it is more efficient for your body to keep them in this shortened state. However, this causes them to feel tight and sore. The same can be said for our anterior chain, consisting of the quads, core and pectorals.

When we find that we have a sore muscle, say our left hamstring, the tendency is for our body to try to compensate by putting more of a load on our left glute. Making it do more of the work. This will then cause an imbalance in our left and right legs which is affecting your gait, form, and efficiency. It's a slippery slope from an imbalance to less effective running and ultimately an injury. It is best to address this initial sore left hamstring before it gets too far down that road. It's actually even better to address these issues before they arise in the first place. Preventative maintenance is far better than rehabilitation.

The main focus of a sports massage is to get these muscles back to their normal lengthened state. A more relaxed condition, where they aren't causing discomfort when running, sitting or walking. Sports massage does this by increasing the blood flow to muscles which helps them repair and recover. It also works out the trigger points in your sore muscles. If you have ever had a sports massage, you know exactly what these trigger points are. When the therapist finds one, you know it.

This is the number one reason why a sports massage isn't the same as a therapeutic, relaxing massage. My recommendation is to add a regular sports massage to your routine. A good sports massage therapist can prevent weeks and months of sitting out of the sport while your body heals from an injury.

FOAM ROLLING

The benefits of foam rolling are much the same as sports massage, just not quite as targeted or as effective. It can act as a good substitute for when you just can't get to the sports massage or if your budget doesn't extend to a monthly visit. One of the best benefits of foam rolling is that you can do it often. By including it in your weekly routine, you can reduce your chances of injury significantly.

REST DAYS

There is a little confusion as to what a rest day should consist of. Many runners consider a rest day to be a day without running. In order for us to get the best benefit from a rest day, it is advisable to make it a day without any exercise that will initiate adaptation. Essentially, a rest day should be a rest day. No running, no gym workouts, no spinning, no swimming. You get the picture. Some easy yoga or stretching is beneficial as is sports massage or other self-care. Just nothing strenuous that may be causing any muscle fatigue.

NUTRITION & HYDRATION

NUTRITION & HYDRATION

IT SHOULD BE obvious that how you fuel your body will either benefit or hinder your performance. Over the course of a 16 week marathon training cycle, nutrition can have a tremendous impact on your race-day peak performance. As with everything involved in marathon training, there are several things to take into account when it comes to nutrition. It isn't always what you consume, but when you consume it that has an impact.

First and foremost, it must be noted that everybody has their own particular limitations when it comes to nutrition. Allergies, intolerances, and even tastes must be taken into account. We will go through the basics of the macronutrients in this section, but when it comes to specific foods, that will be up to the individual.

There are three macronutrients and each of these play a crucial role in running performance. Each has its own unique part to play in providing energy and supporting various physiological processes like muscle growth and vitamin absorption.

Before we get into the specifics, it should be noted that after a running training session, whether it is an intense interval workout, hill repeats or even a long slow distance run, it is best practise to ensure you consume something that includes a good balance of carbs, protein and healthy fats. This should be consumed within one hour of finishing. Your body is in an ideal position to take in these macronutrients at this time.

CARBOHYDRATES

Carbohydrates, (carbs), are the primary fuel source for endurance runners. They are stored as glycogen in the muscles and liver and can be quickly accessed for energy while running. Consuming carbs before and during longer running sessions will help maintain blood glucose levels, delay fatigue and improve endurance performance. Therefore, consuming carbs before a run, particularly long runs, is essential to provide your body with the necessary fuel to sustain exercise. Carbs can also be consumed during longer runs, often in the form of gels, sports drinks or snacks to help maintain energy levels.

Depending on how much time there is between the time carbs are consumed and the time the athlete runs will determine the best type of carbohydrate to have. The further away from the run, the more low GI carbs will be of benefit because they take longer to break down. Examples of low GI carbs would be fruits and berries, vegetables and legumes, brown rice, wholemeal bread, dairy, soy, and whole grain pasta.

If exercise is to take place within 2 hours, then higher GI carbs would be more useful as they are more quickly turned to energy. Examples of these would be white bread, rice, potatoes, sweet potatoes, and breakfast cereals.

PROTEIN

Protein is important for repairing and building muscle tissue. When you run, your muscles are constantly working and, if training particularly hard, will experience micro-tears that need to be repaired, this is part of the adaptation process. Consuming protein after running will help to make these repairs and improve recovery. Runners often focus so much on carbs for fuel that we neglect to consume enough protein on a daily basis. Protein is essential for all athletes in the adaptation process, making us stronger and faster. It is, after all, the way we improve in the sport. If we don't fuel for growth, we don't make the most of our training.

As mentioned above, protein should be consumed as soon as possible after your hard running sessions whether they are speed workouts or long-distance endurance workouts. It is recommended that some protein is consumed within the first hour after exercise to get the most benefits. As a guide, take 20% of your body weight in pounds and consume that many grams of protein for the greatest effect as a recovery meal. For an athlete weighing 150 lbs, that would amount to 30g of protein as a post session recovery meal.

It should also be noted that protein should also be consumed throughout the day as part of a healthy diet, not just after exercise. This is especially true for athletes. Another guide for runners training for a marathon is to consume 75% of body weight, (pounds), in grams of protein. So, the daily consumption calculation for an athlete weighing 150 lbs would be 150 multiplied by 0.75 which would be 112.5g. Obviously, this is a guide, but my advice is to try to be within 10% of that either way.

FATS

Fats also play an important role for an endurance athlete. They are stored in the body as tissue that can be accessed for energy during exercise when glycogen stores are depleted. Many ultra runners will adapt their bodies to consume fats as fuel for their events, with less emphasis on carbohydrates. For a marathon runner, this is inefficient because burning fat is a slower process than accessing glycogen.

Fats are necessary for the absorption and transportation of fat-soluble vitamins, like vitamins A, D, E and K. These examples of fat-soluble vitamins are essential in keeping an athlete healthy from the start of the training block all the way to the start line of the marathon. Vitamin A for the immune system, D for reduced injuries and increasing muscle strength, E for healthy immune and cardiovascular systems and K for strong bones and a strong cardiovascular system as well.

They are also essential for cell membrane function, nervous system function and as an insulation and protection for organs and tissue. The message here is to not neglect fats. They have a bad reputation because they are so calorie rich, but they are essential for a healthy athlete. It is important to note that not all fats are created equal, and some types of fats are healthier than others. Unsaturated fats, such as those found in nuts, seeds, avocados and oily fish are good examples that should be included as part of a balanced diet.

HYDRATION

The key to hydration is to keep the body well hydrated every day. The ideal amount of water consumption for an endurance athlete will depend on several factors. These include duration and intensity of exercise, environmental conditions and an individual's sweat rate. As a general guide, start with this formula. Take your body weight in pounds and divide it in half. Consume that amount of ounces of water per day. Using our 150 lb athlete as an example once again, they would try to consume 75 ounces (2.2 liters) of water on an average day. This would need to be adjusted for someone whose sweat rate is higher, someone who lives in a hot climate, or someone who does a particularly strenuous job, or when on long run.

Now that we have a guideline for daily water intake, let's look at during your training sessions. Dehydration will not only have detrimental effects on performance, but can be very dangerous for one's health. Dehydration tends to sneak up on an endurance athlete.

There are a few guidelines to follow here. In order to get a good idea of how much water you are sweating out, it's a good idea to weigh yourself before your training session. This will be your starting point. Depending on your exertion, you may require water while you are working out. When you finish, get back on the scale and that will give you an idea of how much water you lost during the session. The idea would be to drink 16 ounces (500ml) of water for every pound of body weight lost.

Another method for checking hydration levels is to do the pee test. Under normal circumstances when properly hydrated, one's urine should be pale yellow in color. The darker the color, the more you need to replenish your fluids. It should never get to the point of being a dark yellow or orange in color.

ELECTROLYTES

One last point to mention is the inclusion of electrolytes in your in-exercise hydration routine and in post-run rehydration. Electrolytes are important for endurance runners because they help regulate fluid balance, nerve function and muscle contractions. During long runs, the body loses electrolytes through sweat, which can lead to dehydration, muscle cramping, and a much impaired performance. Therefore, it is important to replenish electrolytes during and after exercise.

The main electrolytes lost through sweat are sodium, potassium and magnesium. Sodium is the most important electrolyte to replace during exercise because it helps maintain fluid balance and prevents hyponatremia (low sodium levels). Potassium and magnesium are also important for muscle and nerve function.

To replenish these electrolytes, endurance runners should consume sports drinks or electrolyte tablets. Sports drinks typically contain a mixture of electrolytes and carbohydrates, which addresses three important issues, fluids, electrolytes and energy stores. After a long run or a hard session where an athlete experiences sweat loss these electrolytes can be replenished with foods high in these micronutrients such as bananas, spinach, avocados and nuts. Many athletes will also take a sports drink immediately after such a difficult session.

It is important to note that similar to hydration, electrolyte needs can vary widely depending on an individual's sweat rate, environmental conditions and exercise intensity. It is a good idea to test out any nutrition and hydration strategies long before race day. Ensure your race fuelling suits your body and the timing is right. If you feel extremely thirsty or are experiencing muscle cramps, it may be too late to salvage your target time. Try to get the water, sports drinks and nutrition into you before you need it.

PREPARING NUTRITIONALLY FOR RACE DAY

You will want to prepare for race day early in your training when it comes to nutrition. I suggest doing a little research well before the event as to where you will eat your evening meal the night before. This is a key meal and it is not the time to try the bacon double cheeseburger if you've not trained by having it the night before a long run. If you are unfamiliar with the location of the race you are taking part in, do some searching on the internet for restaurant recommendations or look into the restaurant at the hotel you are staying in. Check menus to ensure that the foods you are eating prior to your training long runs are available to you. Practice eating this type of food, as close to the local menu as you can get.

In addition to getting the food right, consider making a reservation early at your chosen restaurant the evening before your race. Not only does the right food matter, but the right time to eat matters. It doesn't have to be an exact science, but the closer to your routines you can get, the better and more comfortable you will find it come race day morning.

This is a lesson I learned the hard way. In 2019 I was on the brink of breaking 3 hours for the first time. I was in the best shape of my life. My training had gone extremely well and confidence was high. I traveled to Chester with a large group and to accommodate everyone, we booked a large table at an Italian restaurant for 8pm. By the time everyone ordered and we had our drinks and appetizers eaten, the main course wasn't out until after 9pm. I was used to having a pizza as a pre-long run meal. On this night, I decided to go with a pepperoni pizza. I ate later than normal and my pizza, although extremely tasty, was greasy. I was so hungry that I greedily gobbled it down.

On the morning of the race, all seemed to be going OK. I was hitting every mile on target. Then mile 16 hit and my stomach mutinied. I never experienced stomach issues while racing before, and this was awful. I managed to hold it together without stopping at the portaloos, but I definitely should have stopped to relieve myself. My stomach was crying for 10 miles. My pace fell off and in those last 10 miles I lost about 8 minutes to finish in 3:06:07. I also spent 10 minutes in the portaloos after crossing the finish line. I experienced cramps like never before. The marathon is hard enough, don't sabotage yourself the night before a race. Plan it properly and stick to the plan. As a side note, I no longer eat pizza before a long run anymore. It is pasta and plain sauce every time now.

GELS & IN RACE NUTRITION

As long as you follow a relatively well balanced and healthy diet, your body will have enough energy for at least an hour of vigorous exercise. Our bodies store this energy in muscles and in the liver. As you expend your energy throughout the day it is important to replenish these stores. However, none of us can run a full marathon in 60 minutes, or just over that. Not even the fastest athletes in the world will have enough energy stores within their body to last the length of a marathon. Therefore, in order to avoid hitting the dreaded wall, you will need to take onboard some nutrition along the way.

Sports nutritionists have developed gels, gel blocks and drinks to serve this purpose over the last number of years. If you use these or are looking to start, then you will need to test a variety and find what works best for you and your gastrointestinal system without causing the kind of distress that I suffered in Chester. The good news is, the options are endless. Some athletes can take sports gels without any issues. Gels can have as much as 30g of carbohydrates and have a combination of faster and slower released sugars.

Obviously, there are other options for on-course fuelling. The key thing to do is to find what works best for you and your stomach. Some alternatives to gels, blocks and sports drinks include:

- Raisins
- Sugary candy (gummy bears for example)
- Fruit
- Granola bars
- Cereal bars

The possibilities are endless. Just remember that it is the carbs you are looking for. Snacks that are low in carbs but high in fats or protein aren't going to fuel you as well as carbs. These macro-nutrients take longer to convert to energy. Whatever you choose to top up your energy store on race day needs to be rehearsed during your training. This is vital.

If you choose something that is too large to carry during your race, a banana or sandwich for example, be sure to recruit some help so that someone can meet you on the course to hand you your nutrition. Only the elites have special tables on which to put their on-course nutrition. Don't leave it to chance. This is such an important part of the race that you will need to plan it precisely. Where and when you take your carbs will matter.

CAFFEINE

Caffeine can help a runner perform better. Try it out and see for yourself. A good strong coffee before a run can make for improvements in your performance. Caffeine helps your focus, performance and even recovery. For me, I always have strong coffee about two hours before a marathon. I take it that early as it can affect people in different ways. Coffee is well known to have a laxative effect. In addition to coffee, some of the gels I use during a race contain 100mg of caffeine in each one. I alternate between a caffeinated gel and non-caffeinated gel with each one. I generally take 4 gels in a cold weather marathon and 5 gels in a warm weather marathon.

Once again, the most important factor in whether or not to use caffeine before or during your race is whether or not your body reacts well to it or not. Test it out well before race day. You should be trying these things out before every long run on your training plan.

ALCOHOL

Alcohol is never a performance enhancer. You will hear stories of people who ran their best 5k completely hung over. Wow, terrific, imagine how well they would have run if they weren't hungover. That said, during the course of your training program, alcohol in moderation won't set you back. It can be said to be relaxing after work. However, my honest advice is to avoid it during your training. It is a small sacrifice and it goes back to the question, 'what are you willing to do to hit your goals?' How important is hitting this goal? If the answer is very important, then 16 weeks is a relatively short amount of time to avoid alcohol. You will be surprised how many additional positive side effects it can bring; improved sleep, better focus, more energy and better athletic performance among them.

BUILDING A POSITIVE MINDSET

POSITIVE MINDSET

BUILDING a positive mindset is one of the most beneficial changes one can make for lives. Working on this aspect has huge potential for runners as well. By using visualization techniques, affirmations and positive self-talk a runner can overcome just about any hardship thrown at them during their 26.2 mile race.

VISUALIZATION

Having a positive mindset is probably the most overlooked area of road racing. We've all seen athletes in other sports, like golf, football, and rugby, deliberately lining up behind the ball and concentrating with laser focus before taking their shot or kick. There is a reason for this. Studies have shown that visualizing every aspect of the process before following through actually increases the chance of execution with a desired outcome. With marathon running we have the ability to increase our chances of executing a desired outcome as well, so why not?

Although it does take some practice, mentally rehearsing your race, in the days and weeks leading up to it, can be the easiest method of performance improvement. The process simply takes conviction and repetition. Building a visualization habit begins with deciding on your goal. As an example, if your goal is to finish under 3 hours in your target marathon you would take the following steps:

- Set a clear goal: "I want to finish the marathon in under 3 hours," or even better, "I want to finish my marathon in 2 hours and 58 minutes."
- Choose a consistent time and place to practice. This could be in the morning before breakfast, just before going to bed at night or for 5 minutes at lunch time.
- Create a quiet environment where you can focus without interruption.
- Close your eyes and visualize running the marathon. This will include as much detail as you know. If you know the course, visualize yourself on all the key parts of the course, running strong,

feeling good, even smiling. See yourself approaching and crossing the finish line and the clock showing your goal time.
- Use all your senses. Visualize the sights, sounds, smells and feelings of the race. Imagine the feel of the pavement under your feet, the sound of the crowds cheering and the taste of your gels or sports drinks. Feel yourself running strong, feeling energized by the crowd, feeling happy and extremely proud when crossing the finish line.
- Practice every day, even more than once a day if you have the time. Visualization is a skill that takes repetition. The more you practice, the more natural and effective it will become.
- Stay positive. It is important to maintain a positive attitude throughout the visualization process. Believe in yourself and your ability to achieve your goal. Focus on the positive feelings that will come when you reach your goal.

Visualization is just one more tool to help reach your goal, but it takes very little effort when compared to the physical training you need.

AFFIRMATIONS

Affirmations are also powerful tools to help reach your marathon goals. Once again, like visualization, it takes a little practice. It's not a physical exercise, but it can make the difference between hitting your goal and just missing out. Getting to the start line healthy, well trained, and full of energy is great, but if you don't think the task ahead of you is achievable, then that will most likely be the case. It's the old saying, "whether you think you can or you can't, you're right." By being committed to your goal from the start of your training, you will set yourself up for a successful outcome.

Affirmations are a specific form of positive self-talk that involves the repetition of positive statements or phrases with the goal of reinforcing a desired mindset or outcome. These are often used to promote self-confidence, motivation and success in a specific area of life. For us marathoners, it may be with our target race. Much like visualization, these should be scheduled into your daily routine, maybe first thing in the morning, or perhaps just before bed. Find a quiet, comfortable spot and repeat to yourself some positive statements related to your goal. Spending two to five minutes per day is all it takes.

If you are short of inspiration for what kinds of declarations to make, here are some examples to try (substitute your target goal finish time. I've used a sub-three hour finish as an example):

- "I am a strong and determined sub-three hour marathoner."
- "I trust my training and preparation and know that I'm ready for this challenge."
- "I am a mentally and physically strong runner and will overcome any obstacles that come my way during the race."
- "My body is capable of running a sub 3-hour pace, and I will push myself to reach this goal."
- "I believe in myself and my abilities, and know that I have what it takes to break the 3-hour barrier."
- "With each passing mile, I become stronger and more focussed, and closer to achieving my goal."
- "I am proud of the progress I've made in my training, and excited to see the results in the race."

These are just some examples. Use some of these or make up your own. The important thing is to build this positive mindset and affirmations are a great place to start.

POSITIVE SELF-TALK

Positive self-talk is similar to affirmations, however, this is less structured. This refers to that little voice in your head that is constantly barraging you with your inner monologue. What many of us don't ever realize is that we have full control over that voice. For a great many of us, it is saying negative things, and maybe has been for a very long time. The constant bombardment of negativity can seriously wear us down and put up obstacles to us reaching our goals. Building a positive mindset can be tough and can take a lot of practice.

The first and most important aspect of positive self-talk is recognizing when our inner voice is being negative. This is when it is important to stop, think, and turn it around. This is used as you make your way through the day. For marathoners, you may start to hear yourself saying how hard the run is feeling, how bad the weather is, or how slow your pace is. This is when it is necessary to turn these thoughts into optimistic and constructive statements. The objective is to build confidence and to reduce stress and anxiety. This doesn't mean you should be telling lies, but rather, putting a positive framework around these negative thoughts. Challenge these self-defeating thoughts with phrases like:

- "I am capable of handling this challenge."
- "I can run through any weather, and have been through worse."
- "I completed this session even though it felt really hard."
- "I'm grateful for being able to run as well as I am."
- "I am strong and my training has been excellent."
- "I am proud of the progress I've made so far."

- "I only have (x) miles left. I can do that in my sleep!"
- "I still feel strong and when I cross the line in 2:59, it will be amazing!"

These positive mindset techniques may sound, and feel, a bit "out-there" at first. Try them out, and stick with them and see what happens. There is no-risk, and it takes less than 10 minutes per day. An added bonus is that it may just trickle over to everyday life where a positive mindset can offer profound, life-changing benefits. These are the types of habits that take little effort and give that little advantage to those who do them consistently.

MENTAL TECHNIQUES - COUNTING YOUR CADENCE

There are a couple of mental exercises that can help during the hard latter miles in a marathon. Counting cadence and using a breathing pattern are both helpful for a few different reasons. Counting cadence is a great way to get some of the miles to tick by. Just count every time your right, (or left), foot hits the ground until you get to 60 and then start over. An added benefit is that it gives you an awareness of the current pace you are running.

Like running with a metronome. If done throughout the course of a race, the brain will get to know when it is off rhythm. It will feel and sound wrong, or at least different from where it was earlier. The ideal cadence, technically, is 180 or more strides per minute. So in 60 seconds your one foot should be hitting the ground as close to 90 times as possible. This cadence is something to work on during your training and when it counts, the cadence will feel, and sound, spot on.

MENTAL TECHNIQUES - USING A BREATHING PATTERN

Using a breathing pattern is another physical activity that will help mentally, even more so when the going gets tough. A breathing pattern consists of taking so many strides per breath in and so many strides per breath out. As a guide, an odd breathing pattern is advised in order for a runner to avoid a stitch or stomach muscle cramps. An example of an odd breathing pattern would be three strides per breath in and 2 strides per breath out. By focusing on a breathing pattern for a number of minutes a good portion of a mile will have passed.

When using a breathing pattern to help alleviate a stitch the aim is to have the last stride on your breath out be on the foot opposite the side where the stitch is. So if the stitch is on the left side, the last breath out should occur when your right foot hits the ground. This has been seen to be a successful method of reducing the length of time suffering.

I have examples of using a breathing pattern on the Achieve Running Club YouTube channel.

RACE WEIGHT

RACE WEIGHT

DETERMINING your ideal race weight is a challenge. It comes with experience, especially when fine-tuning a few pounds up or down. There are some decent formulas that will help a marathon runner start this process. Getting it right can mean finishing your fastest marathon and feeling strong at the end.

THE STILLMAN CALCULATION

Some may have heard of the Stillman height/weight table. Dr. Maxwell Stillman developed a chart that described the ideal weight for men and women of a certain height. This is a highly controversial topic, but this is a good starting point. I suggest using this calculation to begin with and then tweak your weight by a few pounds up and a few pounds down to see what works best. Having the perfect racing weight can mean the difference of several seconds per mile in a race. Now who doesn't want those precious seconds. A 10-pound difference in weight can mean upwards of four and a half minutes in your finish time in a 26.2 mile race.

The Stillman height/weight table uses the following calculations and makes the assumption that everyone is five foot tall or taller.

THE STILLMAN CALCULATION FOR WOMEN

First of all with women, the ideal weight begins at 100lbs (45kg) for the first 5 feet (152.4cm). Then 5lbs (2.3kg) for every additional 1 inch (2.54cm). So, a woman, that is 5 foot 4 inches tall should weigh 120 pounds (54.2kg).

THE STILLMAN CALCULATION FOR MEN

Men will use a slightly different calculation. Starting with the first 5 feet (152.4 cm) begins at 110 lbs (50kg) then add 5.5lbs (2.54kg) per inch after that. So for a man of 5 foot 10 inches tall (177.8 cm), he should weigh 165lbs (75.4kg).

THE STILLMAN CALCULATION FOR LONG DISTANCE ATHLETES

Stillman further argued that long distance runners needed to carry even less weight in order to be at their best. He suggested that endurance athletes needed to be 15% lighter. So, the same 5-foot 4-inch woman, who runs marathons, should be 15% lighter than the prescribed 120 lbs meaning that she would be 102 lbs (45.9 kg) and our 165 lb man should be 143 lbs (63.79 kg). That sounds a little unhealthy for my liking. I would argue that more muscle, even though a higher body weight will help the athlete finish strong.

Everyone has a slightly different body type, and this will play a role in one's body weight, as will age and lifestyle. I include the Stillman Calculation as a starting point; a guide. In order to determine *your* perfect weight, it is going to take some time to experiment. There is a very fine line between carrying too much muscle or fat that will be slowing you down and having not enough lean muscle to keep you fast. Finding that balance will help enormously in peaking on race day. Muscle is the key.

These figures were also based on elite and high performing professional athletes. Most of us can't consider ourselves in that category Unfortunately, most of us work full-time jobs and run when we can. Aim to be light and strong, whatever weight that is for you. Just know, that a runner will get 2-3 seconds per mile improvement for every pound of body weight they aren't carrying around the course.

A great many of us will never get down to the calculated body weight from that formula. That is not a problem. But there will be a weight that works best for each of us as an individual. Find yours and you'll have another string to your bow. It does not mean that the lower your weight, the better you'll run. If you don't maintain a healthy weight and muscle mass, your body will break down before you ever reach the finish line.

Just to put this in perspective, I'll share my experience. I'm 5 feet 10 inches tall. In the spring of 2022, at the age of 53, I weighed in at 157 lbs and ran a 3:00:29 marathon in Manchester, England. This is known as a really good, fast course. Then in the summer of the same year, I was down to 154 lbs and ran a 2:58:33. Later in the year, running in Berlin, my weight was even lower at 148 lbs. My lower back and legs were sore from early on, and I ran a 3:08:46. Finding the right balance of strength and weight has proven important to me. In London 2023, weighing in at 152, it felt right. I finished in 2:56:44. I was lean and strong without carrying too much muscle or fat. This seems to be my ideal marathon racing weight.

HOW AND WHEN TO LOSE WEIGHT

I am a firm believer in being at the right race weight as described above. Knowing that you want to be at a specific weight makes the how and when a little easier to figure out. I'll offer a real-life example. At the end of October of 2022, I just finished the Dublin Marathon weighing in at 154 lbs. It was a particularly long year of training and racing, having taken part in four marathons. I was tired both physically and mentally. I took a break from racing and backed off my training. This was also a time to stop eating so carefully. I was in my off-season. By the time New Years Day came around, I had gained 12 lbs and was up to 166.

This gave me 16 weeks to lose 14 lbs and get myself down to my ideal racing weight for race day. However, I find it useful to be a couple of pounds under that target the week before and actually put a couple of pounds back on in the days leading up to race day. This gives me the feeling that I'm getting stronger and replenishing muscle and energy and I'm ready on race day at the ideal weight.

It takes a great amount of discipline to eat a restricted diet for that amount of time and I found myself having good weeks and bad weeks. In other words, some weeks I was losing more than 1lb and other weeks I was gaining more than 1lb. However, come race week, I had managed to be where I wanted to be. The evening before the big day, I was at my desired weight of 152. When you have goals like that and you hit them, it breeds quite a bit of confidence and self-belief.

This is why it is important to be realistic about your race weight. If I had 20 or more pounds to lose, this may have been a little too much and I may not have had that mental boost of hitting my goal weight. So, make sure your goal race weight is within your capability and really try to achieve it.

I set weekly goals and aim to be as close to them each week as possible. As you see your weight slowly creep down towards your goal weight, take stock and be proud of your commitment and discipline. If you have a bad week and are off your target, you may need to reset your target for the following week, but always be mindful of where you are at in this training block. You will still be able to hit your weight target, but you may need to make more of an effort.

One thing to watch out for is that you are doing this weight loss in a healthy manner. You still need to be building strength. So don't lose too much weight too quickly as this is most likely coming at the expense of your strength and stamina. This is the exact opposite of what you are trying to achieve. When race day comes about, you will hopefully be feeling great in your body, no matter what your weight is. You will be feeling strong, fast and confident.

Some runners will actually end up gaining weight during their training block. It is possible that this is where they need to be. However, beware of the false calories that these fitness apps will give you. I've never heard of anyone who regularly burned 1000 calories on a run and then consumed those extra calories throughout the day, and maintained their weight. These numbers are misleading. Stick with a healthy calorie count for you, personally. Burning all these calories is not a license to consume all the food. Be smart, be vigilant and keep a close eye on how your body burns fuel.

WHEN TO GAIN WEIGHT

There are certain times that a runner may need to gain weight in order to get up to ideal racing weight. This should be done by focusing on gaining muscle. The simple method for doing this is to reverse the advice for losing weight. Strength training, protein intake, good hydration and excellent sleep are the ingredients you will need. The biggest difference will be in daily calories consumed and maintaining a calorie surplus.

A BRIEF DISCUSSION ON BMR (BASAL METABOLIC RATE)

BMR or Basal Metabolic Rate, sometimes referred to as Resting Metabolic Rate (RMR), is a calculation of how much energy your body uses when not doing any exercise. This is a useful calculation when determining a starting point in finding your maintenance calorie requirements. Once the number is calculated, use the scale factor for your activity lifestyle adjustment, (sedentary, lightly active, moderately active, etc...), and move forward from there. This will be how many calories you will use up during the average day. In order to lose weight, aim to be below this. In order to maintain current weight, aim to consume this many calories. Finally, in order to gain weight, consume more calories than this. Experiment by performing a weekly weigh-in and if you are genuinely sticking to your calorie intake, this will give you an indication if you need to adjust up or down.

There are other more scientific approaches to finding your personal BMR, which are more accurate. Some clinics dotted around will hook you up to a machine and test you. However, although more accurate, it is also more costly to get the number. Below is the Mifflin St. Jeor Equation that will give you a good indication of what you need to shoot for. Try this and move forward from there based on results. Whatever method you use, it's a useful number. If you need to put on more muscle, you would consume more calories than your maintenance weight.

Computing your BMR Using the Mifflin St. Jeor Equation

Men: 10 x Weight in KG + 6.25 x Height in CM - 5 x Age in Years + 5 = BMR

Women: 10 x Weight in KG + 6.25 x Height in CM - 5 x Age in Years -161 = BMR

Multiply by scale factor for activity level:
Sedentary *1.2
Lightly active *1.375
Moderately active *1.55
Active *1.725
Very active *1.9

FURTHER ADVICE LEADING TO RACE DAY

TAPERING

FOR MANY MARATHON RUNNERS, the taper is the very end of the Race phase of the plan that they most look forward to. It is the last part of the training cycle where mileage and intensity are generally eased off, giving our body the chance to rebuild. This is probably the most important part to get right as far as *peaking* for race day. This is why it is called the peaking phase.

There are mixed feelings on the taper. Some coaches and online plans will have upwards of a three week taper. This is fine for those looking to simply complete the distance, or maybe carrying some minor injuries or niggles. However, I prefer to give my athletes closer to a 10-day taper. This is not set in stone, and every athlete will be different. Depending on experience and individual circumstances, the plans can change. In a best case scenario, when there has been 14 ½ weeks of solid training, a 10 day taper is ideal.

For one thing, there is very little adaptation from a running session that will take place in the immediate short term. It takes between two and ten days for your body to reap any benefits from a hard session. The more stress it is put under, the longer it takes to adapt. After all, there is a reason marathon programs usually take place over 16 weeks. The cycle works by consistently breaking muscle down and rebuilding stronger. See the illustration for a simplified view of the adaptation process:

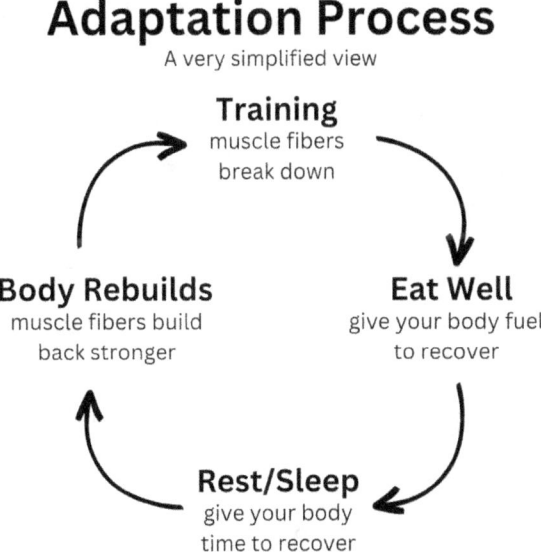

There is a fine line between a taper that is too long and a

taper that is too short. This is why it is tricky to peak for race day. The faster the athlete's times and the more marathons they have run will act as a good guideline for how long the taper should be. In the plans included in this book, there are different tapering strategies deployed and for the purposes of a general plan, the faster the target time, the shorter the taper phase.

PREPARING FOR ALL WEATHER CONDITIONS

16 weeks is a long time to prepare for a race. This will likely mean that the weather in which you train will change considerably from the time you start to the time you reach the start line. The advice I give to my athletes is to prepare for the conditions on the day of the race. Now, there is no possible way to know what the weather will be next week, never mind in four months. But you can give yourself the best chance by preparing for likely scenarios. If you are training through the winter for a spring marathon, then prepare for warmer conditions than you are getting during your training. In other words, for some of your long runs, perhaps put on an extra layer so you are training *hot*. This is particularly important as the spring rolls around and the running weather becomes more ideal. Cooler days, but not cold, are most runners' favorite weather for training. By all means, enjoy these days, but on occasion, put an extra layer on to better prepare for possible hot conditions on race day.

When training *hot*, you must also take onboard more water and nutrition, much like you would if you were racing in the heat. This is the perfect opportunity to practice a race-day water and gel strategy. On the long runs, put out some bottles of water along your route and carry the gels that will be used during the marathon. Alternatively, try a circular route that will bring you around past your car or house a few times where you can leave water and gels. Experiment with your strategy and try different times to drink water and take your nutrition. Not only will you make sure it works during your training, and therefore during your race, but you will be confident that it works. Thus building another mental queue to tell yourself you are on target.

Take the same considerations if the opposite is true. Maybe you are training through the autumn for a winter race. This is actually a little easier to prepare for, because you will be training in warmer conditions than you will have on race day, but you will want to wear the running gear at least a few times before you reach the start line. This will be easier in the weeks leading up to the race. In the days before the marathon, you will get a better idea of what the weather will throw at you, and no matter what it is, you will be able to run your best, because you prepared for it. In this case, remove a layer on the cooler days.

RACE DAY PLANS (PLAN A, PLAN B AND PLAN C)

It is a good idea to have more than one outcome planned for the race. Plan A will be "if things all go my way, what am I capable of?" Plan B will be, "what am I aiming for?" Plan C will be, "what will I be satisfied with?"

Why have three race day plans? You never know what the day will bring. As I keep saying, a marathon program takes a long time to complete. Ideally, at the end of the Race phase of your training, you will hit the start line like a coiled spring, ready to run the best race of your life. However, if the weather doesn't cooperate, or your body doesn't react well to something, or you are starting to come down with a cold or flu, having a Plan C may be the best you have on the day. No matter what happens, you have your experience of the previous 16 weeks in the bank. You will have learned an awful lot about yourself and your body. Take it and move forward, whether it is with a huge personal record or not.

RUNNING WITH A PACER

Should you run with a pacer or not? The answer all depends on who is pacing. Some pacers are good, others not so good. Bigger events will usually have much better pacers than smaller events, but that is a very general statement. My advice is to take the pacer out of your equation and run your own race. Sometimes a pacer can go out fast, banking minutes. Other times they may just get it wrong altogether and need to push the last few miles beyond anyone's physical capability. If you run your own race, at the pace you have decided to run, then nobody else can jeopardize your result. Perhaps stay with the pacer for as long as they keep to your pace and if it changes, either let them go or drop them behind you depending on the situation. Ultimately, you are responsible for running your race and blaming a bad pacer does not change the outcome if it doesn't go to plan.

DETERMINING WHETHER YOU ARE ON TARGET

The best way to determine if you are on target during your race is to set your watch to Average Pace for your run. Mile splits are important, but they will go up and down based on different factors like elevation, water stops, congestion, twists and turns on the course, etc... The only thing that matters is that your overall average pace stays at or below your target pace. As an example, if you want to run a sub-three hour marathon, the overall average pace needs to be 6:51/mile or below. Your previous mile splits mean nothing as long as the overall average is staying under that 6:51/mile. That said, keeping a steady pace is the most efficient way of ensuring success.

Keep in mind also that 6:51/mile is only on target if you run exactly 26.2 miles. Unless you are in a very large marathon, it is unlikely that the marathon line, (the line used to measure the distance), will be visible on the course. Without seeing the line, it is very difficult to run the correct distance. Most of us will end up running closer to 26.4 or even more. That is the reason why it is best to ensure you are a second or two under the target pace.

ADVICE AND TIPS FOR THE WEEK BEFORE RACE DAY

REST

The week prior to race day should have additional rest days. After 15 weeks of hard training, your body needs to be ready for the big event. In the six days leading up to the marathon, I like to give my athletes three complete rest days. Because of this, really good nutrition and hydration habits need to be adhered to. Once again, rest days can have some light yoga or stretching and other self-care. If getting a sports massage, make sure to get it before mid-week. As mentioned, a sports massage can be painful, so it is best to get this done well in advance of the event.

That said, there will still be at least two days of easy running during this week. Possibly something short and sharp the weekend before, but during the week, keep it short and relatively easy. You won't get any benefit from a hard session during this last week on the plan. Let your body rest and heal. That should be the main training goal for week 15.

SLEEP

Sleep in this last week leading into the target marathon is obviously important. Keep focussed on early nights and a good nighttime and morning routine. Come the night before the marathon, many runners will be anxious and sleep may be difficult to find. As long as you are well rested in the week leading up to it, you will be fine. The popular saying is that *it is the night before the night before that matters most.* I agree with that. I have experienced a lack of sleep on the evening before the marathon. It wasn't nearly as detrimental as I thought it would be.

BODY PREPARATIONS

What is meant by body preparations? Well, there are a few things that one can do during the week leading into the target marathon. For one, cut your toenails early in the week. It may even be better to file them. That is simply to avoid cutting them too short and having sore, stingy toes on the morning of the marathon. It also means that your toenails won't be causing any issues in your fast trainers.

This is a time when a reflexology session helps. It is one of the best ways to relax in the lead up to the big day. For those who have never tried it, reflexology is a form of foot massage that focuses on specific reflex points in the foot in order to relieve stress and promote healing in other parts of the body.

For me, it's all about the relaxing effect it promotes in the hours and days after having it done.

Some additional body preparations may be to do some of the aesthetic things to make you feel good and confident. Maybe a haircut. Maybe a manicure, pedicure, or facial. As I mentioned before, when you feel good, you will run well. Confidence is crucial and some self-care will go a long way.

EVENING BEFORE RACE DAY

You are nearly there. With only one more sleep before the big day it is time to really put your racing head on. If you are traveling for your race and staying away from home, make sure you pack your own away bag. Yeah, obviously! Well, once again, I have experience to share. One of my many Dublin Marathon experiences offered me a chance to learn another lesson. Normally, I will always pack everything myself. However, on this occasion I asked my wife to pack my club racing singlet that was in the laundry. She put it in my bag, only for me to arrive on race day to find that the top she packed was hers (she and I ran for the same club, so they looked identical). Now I'm not a particularly large man, but I'm considerably larger than my wife. I pinned the number to the vest and put it on only to feel like The Incredible Hulk! There was no way I was going to be able to wear that top. I had to take one of my t-shirts and cut the sleeves off to make it more like a singlet. I looked like I had been mugged before the race. Lesson learned.

You will want to do the right things to make the race come off to plan and not forget any of the little details. I suggest making a checklist and sticking to it.

- Evening meal booked
- Drop bag packed or ready (details below)
- Morning meal planned and ready to be prepared
- Gels packed and ready
- Any lubrication is laid out and ready
- All racing gear is laid out
- Anything specific to you

PRE-RACE EVENING MEAL

If staying away, perhaps a hotel or guest house, this should have been arranged well ahead of now. If you have a reservation, make sure it was for about 30 minutes before you plan on eating, whatever time you practiced in your training prior to your long runs. The same time, the same foods. If you normally had a glass of wine the night before your long run, have a glass of wine. If you didn't, by all means don't. Don't have the dessert if you haven't had it in training, despite the added carbs. There is a great expression, *the more you carb-load, the more you will need to carb-unload*. Keep things in perspective. Don't overdo it now. More does not always mean better. Trust your training and preparation and don't change things now.

PREPARING YOUR RACE BAG FOR THE BAG DROP

You're almost there. It's time to prepare for the morning. The more you can take care of now, the better and more relaxed your morning will be. Lay out your outfit for the morning. Right down to the socks, underwear, shorts, top(s), and for the male athletes, band-aids to cover your nipples or lube, if that's your anti-chafing method of choice. Get everything ready. Pin your bib number to your top, make sure it is straight and looks good. Remember, *look good, feel good, run good*. You don't want to find yourself short of a few pins, so it is best to do this before you go to bed.

Get your throw away clothes ready, if it is going to be cold before the race starts. Pack your bag with everything you need for after the race. Think carefully about what you put in this bag. This may differ depending on the time of year that your race is occurring.

If the race is taking place on a cold day, you may consider having the following items in your bag:

- A sweatshirt as your body temperature will drop when you finish the race and as it's cold out, you will need something warm to put on
- Warm hat and gloves for the same reason as above

- A rain jacket will be useful in the case of rain. Again, your body temperature will drop when you finish and a cold rain will feel ten times worse after a marathon than on any other day
- Some cash, (or a debit/credit card), just in case you need to get a hot or a cold drink after finishing. You just never know what you may need it for, but it won't take up much space
- A mobile phone. Once again, just in case you need it to find people or directions in an unfamiliar city
- Some snacks as you may feel like you need to replenish your calories soon after completion
- A small bottle of water or a soft drink like a Coke which would be good to replenish the sugars in your system
- Pain killers may just come in handy as well

As for a spring or summer marathon, depending on conditions you may want to include all or some of the above as well as some after sun or sunblock.

YOUR MARATHON DAY & BEYOND

ADVICE AND TIPS FOR RACE DAY

THE TRAINING IS all in the bank and now it's time to execute. Here is some advice leading up to the starting gun and making your way around the course.

WAKE UP

The time has come. You've managed to make it to race day in one piece and feeling like your body is raring to go. One of the most important things on race day is giving yourself more time than you need. You will have practiced this race day ritual by now. Work your wake-up time backwards from the time your race gun goes off. Some of the more local races will likely be easier to get to the start line. Some of the bigger races will require more logistical planning. Either way, get yourself up, showered, fed and ready to go well in advance of the gun going off.

Now is not the time to leave anything to chance. If you are staying in a hotel, go the extra step of arranging a wake up call from the front desk. Don't just rely on your phone for the alarm. Have a backup plan for everything starting with waking up.

BREAKFAST

They say that breakfast is the most important meal of the day. I'm not 100% sure of that, but it most certainly is on this day. Let's say it's a 9am start. You'll want to be eating breakfast, most likely, by 6am. I attended an interview with Mo Farah the morning before the 2023 London Marathon. His advice on breakfast was to eat as much as you can four hours before the race starts. Interesting, for sure, but I don't think I'd do that myself. He and I aren't exactly in the same category as far as athletes go. I like to eat a good sized, but not huge, breakfast, made up of mostly carbohydrates, about three hours before the start. For me personally, my race-day breakfast consists of:

- 60g of porridge oats, with cinnamon, honey, and a little peanut butter
- Two slices of wholegrain toast with peanut butter

- A large, strong black coffee (or two small cups)
- A pint of water

Once I have this in me I'm feeling good and not too full or bloated. Because I've had this breakfast before the last six marathons, I'm confident it will sit well in my stomach and not cause distress.

ARRIVING AT THE START LINE

The only thing to be said about getting to the start line is to leave yourself with enough time to arrive, relaxed, warmed up and well ahead of time. Even in the worst winter conditions, be there early enough to get up towards the front of your wave. In a small marathon, get up as close to the front of your start line as possible. If you are looking for a PR (or PB, depending where you are from), then you should be doing this in a race of any distance. Every second counts when it comes to hitting your target time.

Most races these days will be chip timed with a starting mat. So why should it matter if you are near the front or not? Your time doesn't start until you cross the starting line. Well, this is true, but if you start in the middle of the pack or further back, then you have more runners to get through and more distance to cover as you weave in and out of the pack. OK, you may not want to be on the line with the 2:10 marathoners, but don't be sitting in the middle of the pack. It is your race too, and you've paid your entry fee. Give yourself the best chance to excel as you can. If there are waves, try to get towards the front of yours.

I once missed getting an entry to the Dublin Marathon when the initial entries opened up. The organizers opened up a brief window later in the year and I ended up getting a place during that time. However, it meant I was placed in one of the later waves. When the gun sounded it took me so much time to work my way through the slower runners in the three waves ahead of me. I ended up running well over the 26.2 mile line as well. Wasted energy and wasted time. Don't get caught at the back of a pack.

Another reason for getting to your start line early is that there are normally lines 50 deep at the toilets. If you are there early enough, you can be at the front of those queues and still make it to the front of the starting pack. It's a great time to be surrounded by other runners, all looking to run well and with confidence. It's a time to savor the training you put in. To take stock of the athlete you are. The effort you put in. Be proud of making it to the start line and wish your fellow athletes the best of luck.

FIRST MILE

There is a general perception that one should start off at a relatively easy pace and build up into your race. Many runners adhere to the goal of attempting to run a negative split, where the first half is run slower than the second half of the race. Mile one is almost inevitably going to be faster than what you were hoping to run, especially if you managed to get to the front of your starting wave. With no one in front of you, the adrenaline will be coursing through you and you will be chomping at the bit to get out of the starting pack. By the time you complete the first mile, you should have settled into your goal pace. Don't worry about that fast first mile and stay relaxed.

The same can be said if the first mile was slow. Sometimes we can get caught in a tightly packed starting group. Maybe the streets are narrow and the crowds are big. Don't worry, you should be able to find some space at some point within the first mile and you have 25.2 miles to make up for the lost seconds in the first mile.

SECOND MILE

Your second mile should be where you start setting your pace for the remainder of the race. Keep an eye on your pace here. You know what you are supposed to run for each mile and you should be looking to hit that, or near it, by the end of mile two. If the weather is hot, you may consider starting to take some sips of water at the first water stop, should there be one. If it's not too hot, you may want to wait a mile or two more before you begin taking water.

MILES THREE THROUGH TWELVE

These miles should be feeling relatively steady. No drama. You should be taking small amounts of water at every water stop if it is a hot day, otherwise every 3 miles or so will suffice. Many races only have stops every 5k, so it will depend on the race. Don't over hydrate, but certainly take small amounts throughout the race before you need it.

One thing to be cautious of during these miles is becoming too over-confident. All too often runners will be feeling unusually fresh in these early miles. This encourages them to push the pace a little beyond their training. Stay within your race plans and avoid blowing up later in the race.

HALF-WAY POINT

Now is a good time to self-evaluate. You are probably starting to feel some fatigue. It shouldn't be debilitating, but you know you've been running hard. Maybe you've started taking your on-course nutrition and if not, you should be thinking hard about starting. You will have seen the clock or your watch would have shown you where you are at. At this point it is getting a little late to make serious adjustments, but there is still time to alter your pace. If you are only a minute or two behind your target pace and you feel strong, by all means, chip away. You don't need to make up the time all at once. A few seconds each mile for 13.1 miles will make a big difference. The key is to try to remain steady through the upcoming harder miles.

20 MILES

The marathon race is about to start. This is where all of your positive thinking, visualization and affirmations will be required. This is hard! Racing a marathon is very hard, maybe the hardest thing you've ever done. Don't let the negative thoughts and that inner voice start to take over. Keep that voice at bay by using all of the work you did during your training around positive thinking. Tell yourself you are strong. You can keep this pace up for another 10k. You can run a 10k in your sleep. It's only 6.2 miles.

If you are struggling to stay positive, try some mental games discussed earlier. Counting cadence, following a breathing pattern, or even engaging with the crowd are all ways to make these next few miles tick over. One way or the other you will need to dig deep. Mental strength is a huge benefit here and is the main reason why we practice all of these things early and often in our training.

24 MILES

Here you are, only 2.2 miles to go. You can feel it now. You may have got a second wind after taking the last caffeine gel. You've been taking small amounts of water at each stop, maybe a sports drink if you used them in your training. The end is in sight. It's no longer a question of can you finish, it is a question of will you hit your target. I've seen many marathoners find unbelievable strength and finish the last two miles among the two fastest miles on the day. You can do anything for two miles. This is less than a 5k, much less. This is easy. You are strong. Positive self-talk. Push on!

Your brain will be doing some serious runner's math at this point. Calculating your finish time and re-calculating two or three times. Don't be too concerned if your brain isn't too cooperative with math problems at this point. Most of the blood flow should go to your legs, not your thinking muscle. The positive thing is that as you try to divide the time it takes to complete a mile by how much distance is left, the miles continue to fall behind you.

LAST MILE

This is the moment you've been waiting for. All the work was worth it. Take it all in. The crowds cheering you on in a city marathon will drive you forward. In a smaller marathon, have a peek at your watch and bask in the glory of having done what you set out to achieve. You know for a fact that, whether you have achieved your goal or not, you gave it all and you persevered. Don't slow down despite what your head is telling you. Every second counts. Wouldn't it be a gut punch to just miss your goal by one second? In my first race that I finally flirted with a sub three hour marathon I ran 3:00:29 in the 2022 Manchester Marathon in England. I missed it literally by 30 seconds. I can honestly say I didn't have those 30 seconds in me on that day. I had given it everything. But there is always that doubt. I learned from that experience, as I did from all my 35 marathons.

But back to you. You should be able to see the finish line, like you did countless times in your head while doing your visualization. You can see your watch, just like you did in your mind's eye. You hear the noise, smell the smells as you did with your eyes closed each morning. You've been here before and now it is real. Nobody will ever be able to take this away from you and you proved all the doubters wrong. Congratulations!

Make your way through the finisher's funnel. Receive your medal with pride and thank the volunteers along the way. Congratulate all the other runners who finished in front, beside, and behind. You all did something that very few of us can say we have done.

It is very important at this point to keep moving. If you sit down immediately you will find your heart rate will just drop. This is dangerous. This happened to me on one of the first races I ran when chasing my first Boston Qualifiers. I just completed the Waterford Marathon in 2014 and as soon as I crossed the finish line I stopped and bent over to put my hands on my knees to try to catch my breath. The next thing I knew I was face down on the track. Soon the medical professionals assisted me into a wheelchair. Two hours later I left the medical tent after a number of IV's and some emergency massage therapy to help alleviate leg cramps.

Had I kept upright and walking, things would have been much better. The lesson I learned was don't stop, keep moving, even slowly. Just keep walking for a few minutes to keep the blood flowing. After a few minutes, you should be fine to find a seat or put your legs up against a wall. But just keep moving for a little while longer.

POST MARATHON

EVENING

It will be tempting to get out and celebrate with a few drinks, or maybe a few too many drinks. Just keep in mind what you've just put your body through. You will be doing yourself a big service if you call it an early night without any alcohol. This is hard to do and you may feel this is a bit too far. But your body will need rest and fluids to replenish what you lost on the course. It does not need to be inundated with alcohol causing further dehydration. The more good food and healthy liquids you consume the quicker you will recover. The more rest and recovery you can give your tired body, the quicker you will be back feeling like yourself again. You need not act like a saint, but give it a day or two to get back to some sort of normality before punishing your body. It did amazing things for you on race day. Reward it.

FIRST TWO WEEKS AFTER YOUR MARATHON

You should give yourself a couple of weeks of very little running. When you do feel ready, easy does it. A few easy miles here and there will go a long way. I'd say 20 miles in the following two weeks is plenty and there should be no pacy runs at all. Full recovery mode at this time. If you do it right, there is much more to come. But in these two weeks, rest and recovery is key. Good, healthy nutrition will be your friend.

Too many runners smash their marathon and then go on to abuse their body with the worst food possible. Or maybe over-indulge with alcohol for a couple of weeks. After all, 4 months is a long time to have held back. However, you've put yourself into a great position health wise and it's time to take advantage. Maintain a good sleep pattern, your good positive mental exercise you've started and combined with your good nutrition, you are in line for something amazing.

THREE WEEKS OUT

This is one of the best periods of time on the running calendar. With the lone exception of the target marathon, this is my favorite time in running. Three weeks after running a target marathon you should be very well rested. But you will also have all of the benefits from your rigorous marathon training. Provided you didn't go crazy and gain 15 pounds of body weight from all the celebrations, you should still be fighting fit. Now is the time to find a 5k or a 10k. It will feel like a stroll in the park, but you will fly. Enjoy this brief period of time by nailing some PR's in shorter races. I have ran my best 5k times after a marathon so many times I can't even count them. Get out and enjoy this time because you will need to take some down time from the hard, physical training on the roads.

PICK YOUR NEXT MARATHON TARGET

Give yourself whatever time you need in order to be physically and mentally prepared for another target marathon. Personally, I love running off-plan for about two or three months, but before long I'm ready to get back to the hard training. If you are anything like me, after a spell off plan, you will be feeling like you are getting out of shape, and getting slow. It's not a great feeling when we don't have something to train for, something to look forward to.

Now is also the time to review the plan you followed. Pore through the notes you took in your training log. Determine what went well and what you would change for the next one. You have all the data you need to adjust your plan you did for this marathon in order to improve even more on the next one. There is always a Next One.

THE PLANS

THE PLANS INCLUDED in this book range from breaking the 4-hour mark all the way down to finishing under 2:45 and every 15 minutes in between. When choosing the right plan for you, first know that you must commit to the plan. From sub-4 through 3:15 the plans cover medium mileage, where sub-3 and 2:45 are high mileage plans. All of these plans require a huge commitment in time, effort and sacrifice to your daily routines. However, by following one of these, and if you are able to hit all the session targets, or at least most of them, you will reach your goals. These have been tried and tested over several years, with many athletes, running different courses.

Included in each week of your plan will be some coaching points where you will be asked to work on some aspect of running. All of the advice will come together in the final week and pay dividends in your target marathon.

Each of these plans is hard, but in the end, nothing worthwhile has ever come easy. It's your turn to do something you never thought possible.

GUIDE TO DIFFERENT SESSION PACES

Most of the sessions on these plans will refer to a relative pace. Every plan will have easy runs but an easy run for a sub four hour finish will be slower than an easy run for a sub three runner. Here is a guide to judge your pace on each of these relative sessions.

LSD: This is a Long Slow Distance run. This should be between 90 seconds - 2 minutes slower than target marathon pace. Very comfortable and conversational. This will be the slowest paced run of the week. This run is the one that most advanced marathoners get wrong. It is the reason really good runners fail to hit their goals in this distance. This is so often executed incorrectly, that I've included an extended explanation. So please read the detailed description below on executing the Long Slow Distance Run.

It is important to do at least some of your long slow distance runs on your own. When you are racing your goal marathon, you will not be chatting to those around you for all 26.2 miles. It is a good idea to get used to the loneliness of all those miles.

Spending these hours by yourself will be good mental preparation and come race day, you will have already got to know that little voice in your head a little more intimately.

Easy Run: This pace is conversational and should feel easy. No trouble breathing, no trouble speaking in full sentences. This will probably be 60-90 seconds slower than marathon race pace.

Keep in mind that easy runs are the perfect time to work on improving your running technique. Pick a certain aspect of your running form that you can improve on, and work on that for a few weeks at a time. By making good form and technique a habit, you will find these habits carry over to race day.

Some examples of good form and technique to work on include:

- Running tall, with relaxed shoulders that are held back and down in your stance
- Running with high hips, pretending you have a bowl of water between your hips and you don't want to spill any
- A forefoot strike
- Good push off your toes with each stride
- Knee lift, particularly up hills
- Good arm drive, particularly up hills or when tired
- Keeping your head up, with your gaze looking forward at the ground about 30 yards in front. A

good visual is pretending you have an orange held under your chin
- Keeping your whole body relaxed, not carrying tension anywhere

Steady Run: The steady state run should be run comfortably hard. It is run at a good hard effort, but not race pace. Conversation is more difficult and short sentences are possible. Typically 30-45 seconds slower than marathon race pace.

Progression Run: The goal of a progression run is to run each mile faster than the previous mile. This is excellent for getting better acquainted with running by feel. These can be fun and challenging.

Hilly Run: This is a session run over a course that has a few good hard hills in it. It's not a hill repeat session, but is more of preparation for a real course where hills need to be traversed.

Hill Repeats: These are run on longer hills that take up to 90 seconds to get from the bottom to the top. Run up and jog down for recovery before turning around and running up again. There will be recovery periods between sets, but not between reps. These are not sprints. We are marathoners, not sprinters. Complete them at a steady pace and effort level.

All Other Sessions: All other sessions will have target paces set. For intervals, the goal is to run each rep at the same pace as the previous one. Avoid going too fast for the first few at the expense of the effort on the latter reps. Don't be overly concerned about using a track for interval sessions. These can be executed just as successfully on a flat road.

No Running Days: On these no running days, it is OK to cross train and do strength training, just don't carry out any running sessions.

Rest Days: Rest days are exactly that, rest days. Stretching and yoga are advisable, but otherwise, nothing. This is the time for the body to catch up on repairs.

EFFECTIVELY EXECUTING THE LONG SLOW DISTANCE RUN

Even for those who know what it is, there is a lot of confusion around how to execute it. The biggest mistake so many runners make is that they do their LSD at too fast a pace. Running sessions are structured on a plan in order to achieve a specific desired adaptation. The long slow distance run has so many benefits, even on top of the endurance it builds, that it would be wrong to just call it an endurance session. Endurance, aerobic capacity, mental fitness, injury prevention, strength and even enjoyment are some of the outcomes of the LSD.

First and foremost the long slow distance run is an endurance session. It improves our ability to maintain a race pace for a longer period of time. Whatever the race distance, building up the time on feet, will help a runner remain strong towards the finish line. Gradually increasing your LSD throughout the training block, allows your body to adapt and to run for longer. The addition of speed work combined with the long slow run is where the magic happens. The problem with many runners is they do their LSD's too pacy. This goes against the desired outcome of the session. The ideal pace should be somewhere between 90 seconds to 2 minutes slower per mile than race pace. The more time on your feet, the greater the workout you are giving your muscles. As with any sport, along with proper rest and nutrition, the more you work, the stronger you get.

The long slow distance run is also a great way to build aerobic capacity. It should generally remain in zone two heart rate range and therefore is strictly an aerobic workout. Your heart and lungs are like a pump and an air filter. Long slow distance runs help your heart become better at pumping blood and your lungs get better at taking up oxygen. This means you can get more oxygen to your muscles when you need it. This is one of the main desired outcomes of this session. Doing your LSD at a faster pace isn't going to improve these functions as well as a slower run will.

Doing your Long Slow Runs at a nice easy "conversation" pace improves mental fitness as well as enjoyment. OK, these two things may seem to conflict, but bear with me. These can be incredibly hard sessions. After all, not many runners see a

20 mile run on their training plan and really look forward to it? Some of us do, but I'd say we are few and far between. So we know they are mentally tough. However, when a long, slow run is complete the feeling is quite amazing. By completing these hard runs we callous the brain just that little bit more. We are able to withstand those hours on our feet. When race day comes around and we are getting into those last few miles, we have these LSD's in the bank.

As for enjoyment, well these runs can be a shared hell, if that makes sense. When we do these long slow distance runs as part of a training group, we are all in it together. At a conversation pace, the company can be very much appreciated. It's a chance to get to know other runners and to share advice and concerns. So, the lesson here is to keep a positive mindset on your long slow distance runs. They can be enjoyable.

We all know that mixing things up in training is a best practice for injury prevention. There are speed workouts on the track. Some fast runs on the road will work on speed endurance. Adding in your weekly long slow distance run, at conversation pace, is just another pace to the mix. You won't be overextending yourself during these runs making them far less likely to cause an injury. On top of that, these are good, productive miles to add to your weekly load. The concept of easy runs easy and hard runs hard is key here. By sticking to that mantra you will reduce your injury risk.

This is a great time to focus on good running form too. It

is so much easier to practice all the basics of good running form, drilling it into your technique. Because the pace is slower, there is more time to focus on posture, foot-strike, head position, etc... Everything that makes running more efficient and easier.

There is a time for race pace workouts, even race-pace long runs, just not the LSD sessions. This is probably a coach's most difficult concept to get through to athletes. The world's greatest marathon runner of all time runs 13 sessions per week. Of these, between 70-80% of these runs are upwards of 2 minutes/k slower than race pace. If that doesn't prove it, nothing will. You run slow in order to race fast. Improving is a process and your body adapts to the workouts it is given. Stick to the LSD concept, SLOW DOWN, and focus on your ultimate goal, your marathon not the pace of your long slow run.

A BRIEF NOTE ABOUT RUNNING BY FEEL

Very much like heart rate training, I use relative paces for many sessions on the plan. These are the easy and steady runs. I use these because sometimes we just don't feel great on a session, while other times a specific pace feels too easy. By using relative paces, the objective is to get the session done within an effort level. This is running by feel.

A very useful tool to judge the relative pace is to use your breathing patterns (as discussed at the end of Chapter 6, under Mental Techniques). An easy run should be kept at a pace where you can run at a 3-4 or 3-3 pattern, similar to heart rate zone 2 to 3. Whereas a steady run would be a 2-3 or a 2-2 pattern, similar to a heart rate zone 3 to 4. Whatever method you use to determine your easy and steady pace, the goal is to keep it at that effort level.

DIGITAL PLAN TEMPLATES

Unfortunately, the format of a printed book, or an ebook, does not lend itself to the training log I developed. It is designed as a Google Sheet, (or an alternative Excel spreadsheet), with all the formulas and the ability to log every single piece of data necessary for a runner.

However, I have made these templates, one for each of the plans included in this book, available at a discount for those who have purchased this book. These can be found at https://achieverc.com/downloads/ and use discount code: **MTS_BPD** to get your reader discount off the list price. These are big spreadsheets with a lot of information being captured. They have been a big help to me and I know you will like using them too, especially if you are a data nerd like myself.

PERSONAL COACHING

SOME RUNNERS NEED that extra little push in order to stay true to their plans. Someone to hold them accountable. Someone to adjust their plans when injuries and niggles start appearing. Someone to answer questions on a daily or weekly basis and explain the ins-and-outs of the training.

Discover a personalized approach to elevate your running journey with my coaching services. Embrace a monthly coaching package featuring comprehensive support: receive weekly training updates, engage in regular video call check-ins, and access unlimited guidance to address all your inquiries and worries. While books and guides provide valuable insights, nothing parallels the impact of individualized coaching. Benefit from tailored training plans geared towards specific races or maintaining peak performance between events. Explore your diverse coaching options today at https://jmruncoach.com/services.

If you are ready to elevate your running and crush new personal records then sign up today. Or you can also reach out to me at John McDonnell Running Coach on Facebook and we can discuss your goals and how I can help you reach them. I am also contactable by email at john@jmruncoach.com.

SUB 4:00 PLAN - MEDIUM MILEAGE PLAN

Sub 4 Hour

Week 1 - Total Weekly Mileage: 24

Coaching Points: Work on doing some balance exercises every day, just a few minutes of standing on one leg per day, throughout the day.

Focus on good running form, especially on the easy and steady runs. Running tall, chest forward with shoulders relaxed and down in your posture.

Monday - 5 miles easy
Tuesday - No running
Wednesday - No running
Thursday - 6 miles easy

Friday - Rest day
Saturday - 3 miles steady
Sunday - 10 miles LSD

Sub 4 Hour
Week 2 - Total Weekly Mileage: 27
Coaching Points: Work on doing some balance exercises every day, just a few minutes of standing on one leg per day, throughout the day.

Focus on good running form, especially on the easy and steady runs. Running tall, chest forward with shoulders relaxed and down in your posture.

Monday - 5 miles easy
Tuesday -

- 1 mile easy
- 2 sets of 6 x 60 second hill repeats. No recovery between reps and 90 seconds between sets
- 1 mile easy

Wednesday - No running
Thursday - 4 miles easy
Friday - Rest day
Saturday - 3 miles steady

Sunday - 11 miles LSD

Sub 4 Hour
Week 3 - Total Weekly Mileage: 29
Coaching Points: Work on doing some balance exercises every day, just a few minutes of standing on one leg per day, throughout the day.

Focus on good running form, especially on the easy and steady runs. Running tall, chest forward with shoulders relaxed and down in your posture.

Monday - 5 miles easy
Tuesday - 4 mile hilly run
Wednesday - No running
Thursday - 5 miles easy
Friday - Rest day
Saturday - 3 miles steady
Sunday - 12 miles LSD

Sub 4 Hour
Week 4 - Total Weekly Mileage: 33
Coaching Points: Work on doing some balance exercises every day, just a few minutes of standing on one leg per day, throughout the day.

Focus on good running form, especially on the easy and steady runs. Running tall, chest forward with shoulders relaxed and down in your posture.

Monday - 4 miles easy
Tuesday - 5 miles steady
Wednesday - No running
Thursday - 6 miles steady
Friday - Rest day
Saturday - 5 miles steady
Sunday - 13 miles LSD

Sub 4 Hour
Week 5 - **Total Weekly Mileage: 37**
Coaching Points: Work on doing some balance exercises every day, just a few minutes of standing on one leg per day, throughout the day.

Focus on good running form, especially on the easy and steady runs. Running tall, chest forward with shoulders relaxed and down in your posture. With 4 weeks of good running form, good habits will start to be ingrained. Keep a good focus on these things.

Now is a good time to start looking at cadence. The technical running model calls for a cadence of at least 180 strides per minute. Look at your stats from your running sessions and if you are under this average on your runs, particularly your steady and faster runs, it is time to work on arm-drive. Your arm swing determines how fast your legs turnover. Start here by driving your arms faster and with purpose, this will increase your cadence naturally. Try to increase your cadence, even slightly each week, over the next weeks.

Monday - 5 miles easy
Tuesday

- 1 mile warm up
- 3 sets of 4 x 90 seconds hill repeats. No recovery between reps and 90 seconds between sets
- 2 miles easy

Wednesday - No running
Thursday - 5 miles steady
Friday - 3 miles easy
Saturday - 4 miles steady
Sunday - 15 miles LSD

Sub 4 Hour
Week 6 - Total Weekly Mileage: 39
Coaching Points: Work on doing some balance exercises

every day, just a few minutes of standing on one leg per day, throughout the day.

Good relaxed running form should be coming naturally.

Continue working on cadence by working your arm drive. Keep a close eye on your running stats and look to make progress each week.

Monday - 5 miles easy
Tuesday

- 1 mile easy
- 3 sets of 4 x 400m repeats
- 200m slow active recovery between reps
- 2 minutes between sets
- Target pace per rep: 105-110 seconds
- 1 mile easy

Wednesday - No running
Thursday - 7 miles easy
Friday

- 1 mile easy
- 3 miles @ 8:20/mile pace
- 1 mile easy

Saturday - 5 miles steady
Sunday - 12 miles LSD

Sub 4 Hour
Week 7 - Total Weekly Mileage: 34
Coaching Points: Work on doing some balance exercises every day, just a few minutes of standing on one leg per day, throughout the day.

Good relaxed running form should be coming naturally.

Continue working on cadence by working your arm drive. Keep a close eye on your running stats and look to make progress each week.

Monday - 3 miles easy
Tuesday

- 4 miles progression run
- First mile @ 8:30/mile pace
- Last mile @ 7:40/mile

Wednesday - No running
Thursday - 5 miles easy
Friday - No running
Saturday

- 1 mile easy
- 4 miles @ 8:20/mile pace
- 1 mile easy

Sunday - 16 miles LSD

Sub 4 Hour
Week 8 - **Total Weekly Mileage: 41**
Coaching Points: Work on doing some balance exercises every day, just a few minutes of standing on one leg per day, throughout the day.

Good relaxed running form should be coming naturally.

Continue working on cadence by working your arm drive. Keep a close eye on your running stats and look to make progress each week.

Monday - 5 miles easy
Tuesday

- 1 mile easy
- 2 sets x 3 reps x 800m repeats
- 200m slow active recovery between reps
- 2 minutes static recovery between sets
- Target each rep: 3:55-3:40/rep

- 1 mile easy

Wednesday - Rest day
Thursday - 6 miles steady
Friday - Rest day
Saturday - 7 miles easy
Sunday - 18 miles LSD

Sub 4 Hour
Week 9 - **Total Weekly Mileage: 42**
Coaching Points: Work on doing some balance exercises every day, just a few minutes of standing on one leg per day, throughout the day.

Good relaxed running form should be coming naturally.

Continue working on cadence and working on your arm drive. Look at your stats from your running sessions and if you still need work, we can try another method. I'm not one to listen to music when I run, but it is a good way to work on cadence. So if you are not making progress, try running with music, but ensure your playlist has songs with 180 beats per minute. There are plenty of playlists out there that are designed for this.

Monday - 4 miles easy

Tuesday - 8 miles hilly run
Wednesday - No running
Thursday - 6 mile progression up to 8:00/mile for last mile
Friday - Rest day
Saturday - 9 miles steady
Sunday - 15 miles LSD

Sub 4

Week 10 - **Total Weekly Mileage: 45**

Coaching Points: Work on doing some balance exercises every day, just a few minutes of standing on one leg per day, throughout the day.

Good relaxed running form should be coming naturally.

Continue working on cadence and working on your arm drive and possibly listening to 180 beats per minute playlists.

Monday - 3 miles easy
Tuesday - 6 miles @ 8:45/mile pace
Wednesday

- 1 mile easy
- 4 x 1200m repeats
- 200m slow active recovery between reps
- Target each rep: 5:45 - 6:00 / rep

- 1 mile easy

Thursday - 6 miles easy
Friday - Rest day
Saturday

- 1 mile easy
- 3 miles @ 8:45/mile
- 1 mile easy

Sunday - 20 miles LSD

Sub 4 Hour
Week 11 - Total Weekly Mileage: 34
Coaching Points: Work on doing some balance exercises every day, just a few minutes of standing on one leg per day, throughout the day.

Good relaxed running form should be coming naturally.

Continue working on cadence and working on your arm drive and possibly listening to 180 beats per minute playlists.

Monday - 5 miles easy
Tuesday

- 1 mile easy
- 5 miles @ 8:40/mile pace
- 1 mile easy

Wednesday - Rest day
Thursday - 5 miles easy
Friday - No running
Saturday - 4 miles steady
Sunday - 13 miles LSD

Sub 4 Hour
Week 12 - **Total Weekly Mileage: 39**
Coaching Points: Work on doing some balance exercises every day, just a few minutes of standing on one leg per day, throughout the day.

Good relaxed running form should be coming naturally.

Continue working on cadence and working on your arm drive and possibly listening to 180 beats per minute playlists.

Monday - 5 miles easy
Tuesday - Rest day
Wednesday

- 1 mile easy

- 4 x 1 mile repeats @ 7:40/mile pace
- 2 minutes slow jog recovery between reps
- 1 mile easy

Thursday - 5 miles easy
Friday - No running
Saturday - 5 miles steady
Sunday - 18 miles LSD

Sub 4 Hour
Week 13 - Total Weekly Mileage: 45
Coaching Points: Work on doing some balance exercises every day, just a few minutes of standing on one leg per day, throughout the day.

Good relaxed running form should be coming naturally. Cadence should be better than when you started.

Now we will start focussing on mental strength. As we approach the final Race Phase of the plan, it is time to really focus on positive self-talk, visualization, and affirmations. Reinforce all the work you've done but ensuring no negative thoughts or doubts slip into your head. Zero negativity!

Monday - 5 miles easy
Tuesday

- 1 mile easy
- 4 miles @ 8:20/mile
- 1 mile easy

Wednesday - Rest day
Thursday - 7 miles steady
Friday - No running
Saturday - 5 miles easy
Sunday

- 10 miles @ 8:50/mile
- + 12 miles LSD
- Complete this as a single run

Sub 4 Hour

Week 14 - Total Weekly Mileage: 32

Coaching Points: Work on doing some balance exercises every day, just a few minutes of standing on one leg per day, throughout the day.

Good relaxed running form should be coming naturally. Cadence should be better than when you started.

Stay positive, practice daily positive self-talk, visualization and affirmations. Self-belief is key. You have earned your upcoming personal record.

Monday - 3 miles easy

Tuesday

- 1 mile easy
- 5 x 1k reps
- 200m active slow jog recovery between reps
- Target rep each: 4:45-4:55
- 1 mile easy

Wednesday - 3 miles easy

Thursday - Rest day

Friday

- 1 mile easy
- 4 miles @ 8:20/mile
- 1 mile easy

Saturday - No running

Sunday

- 7 miles @ 8:40/mile
- + 8 Miles LSD
- Complete this as a single run

Sub 4 Hour
Week 15 - Total Weekly Mileage: 30

Coaching Points: Work on doing some balance exercises every day, just a few minutes of standing on one leg per day, throughout the day.

Good relaxed running form should be coming naturally. Cadence should be better than when you started.

Stay positive, practice daily positive self-talk, visualization and affirmations. Self-belief is key. You have earned your upcoming personal record.

Monday - 5 miles easy
Tuesday

- 1 mile easy
- 2 miles @ 8:10/mile
- 1 mile easy

Wednesday - Rest day
Thursday - 5 miles easy
Friday - Rest day
Saturday

- 1 mile easy
- 1 mile @ 8:10/mile
- 1 mile easy

Sunday - 13 miles LSD

Sub 4 Hour
Week 16 - Total Weekly Mileage: 34.2
Coaching Points: You have arrived at race week. Everything will come together this week. Trust your training. Trust yourself and your coach. You have put in all the work. Now all you need to do is stay positive, keep the positive self-talk working in your favor and execute your race plan.

Monday - Rest day
Tuesday

- 1 mile easy
- 1 mile @ 8:10/mile
- 1 mile easy

Wednesday - Rest day
Thursday - 3 miles easy
Friday - Rest day
Saturday - 2 miles very easy
Sunday - RACE DAY (26.2 miles)

Target Pace: 8:55/mile

SUB 3:45 PLAN - MEDIUM MILEAGE PLAN

3:45 Plan

Week 1 - Total Weekly Mileage: 26

Coaching Points: Work on doing some balance exercises every day, just a few minutes of standing on one leg per day, throughout the day.

Focus on good running form, especially on the easy and steady runs. Running tall, chest forward with shoulders relaxed and down in your posture.

Monday - 5 miles easy
Tuesday - No running
Wednesday - No running
Thursday - 6 miles easy

Friday - Rest day
Saturday - 5 miles steady
Sunday - 10 miles LSD

3:45 Plan
Week 2 - Total Weekly Mileage: 30
Coaching Points: Work on doing some balance exercises every day, just a few minutes of standing on one leg per day, throughout the day.

Focus on good running form, especially on the easy and steady runs. Running tall, chest forward with shoulders relaxed and down in your posture.

Monday - 5 miles easy
Tuesday

- 1 mile easy
- 2 sets of 6 x 60 second hill repeats. No recovery between reps and 90 seconds between sets
- 1 mile easy

Wednesday - No running
Thursday - 5 miles easy
Friday - Rest day
Saturday

- 1 mile easy
- 3 miles @ steady
- 1 mile easy

Sunday - 11 miles LSD

3:45 Plan

Week 3 - Total Weekly Mileage: 32

Coaching Points: Work on doing some balance exercises every day, just a few minutes of standing on one leg per day, throughout the day.

Focus on good running form, especially on the easy and steady runs. Running tall, chest forward with shoulders relaxed and down in your posture.

Monday - 5 miles easy
Tuesday - 4 mile hilly run
Wednesday - No running
Thursday - 6 miles easy
Friday - Rest day
Saturday

- 1 mile easy
- 3 miles steady
- 1 mile easy

Sunday - 12 miles LSD

3:45 Plan
Week 4 - **Total Weekly Mileage: 37**
Coaching Points: Work on doing some balance exercises every day, just a few minutes of standing on one leg per day, throughout the day.

Focus on good running form, especially on the easy and steady runs. Running tall, chest forward with shoulders relaxed and down in your posture.

Monday - 4 miles easy
Tuesday

- 1 mile easy
- 3 sets of 4 x 90 second hill repeats. No recovery between reps and 90 seconds between sets
- 1 mile easy

Wednesday - No running
Thursday

- 1 mile easy
- 4 miles steady
- 1 mile easy

Friday - 3 miles easy

Saturday

- 1 mile easy
- 3 miles steady
- 1 mile easy

Sunday - 13 miles LSD

3:45 Plan

Week 5 - Total Weekly Mileage: 38

Coaching Points: Work on doing some balance exercises every day, just a few minutes of standing on one leg per day, throughout the day.

Focus on good running form, especially on the easy and steady runs. Running tall, chest forward with shoulders relaxed and down in your posture. With 4 weeks of good running form, good habits will start to be ingrained. Keep a good focus on these things.

Now is a good time to start looking at cadence. The technical running model calls for a cadence of at least 180 strides per minute. Look at your stats from your running sessions and if you are under this average on your runs, particularly your steady and faster runs, it is time to work on arm-drive. Your arm swing determines how fast your legs turnover. Start here by driving your arms faster and with purpose, this will increase your cadence naturally. Try to increase your cadence, even slightly each week, over the next weeks.

Monday - 5 miles easy
Tuesday - Rest day
Wednesday - 3 miles hilly
Thursday

- 5 miles progression
- First mile @ 8:45/mile pace
- Last mile @ 7:30/mile

Friday - 6 miles easy
Saturday - 4 miles steady
Sunday - 15 miles LSD

3:45 Plan
Week 6 - **Total Weekly Mileage: 39**
Coaching Points: Work on doing some balance exercises every day, just a few minutes of standing on one leg per day, throughout the day.

Good relaxed running form should be coming naturally.

Continue working on cadence by working your arm drive. Keep a close eye on your running stats and look to make progress each week.

Monday - 5 miles easy

Tuesday

- 1 mile easy
- 3 sets x 4 reps x 400m repeats
- 200m slow active recovery between reps
- 2 minutes between sets
- Target pace per rep: 100-105 seconds
- 1 mile easy

Wednesday - No running

Thursday - 7 miles easy

Friday

- 1 mile easy
- 3 miles @ 7:50/mile pace
- 1 mile easy

Saturday - 5 miles steady

Sunday - 12 miles LSD

3:45 Plan

Week 7 - **Total Weekly Mileage: 38**

Coaching Points: Work on doing some balance exercises every day, just a few minutes of standing on one leg per day, throughout the day.

Good relaxed running form should be coming naturally.

Continue working on cadence by working your arm drive. Keep a close eye on your running stats and look to make progress each week.

Monday - 3 miles easy

Tuesday

- 4 miles progression run
- First mile @ 8:20/mile pace
- Last mile @ 7:30/mile

Wednesday - No running

Thursday - 5 miles steady

Friday - 4 miles easy

Saturday

- 1 mile easy
- 4 miles @ 7:50/mile pace
- 1 mile easy

Sunday - 16 miles LSD

3:45 Plan
Week 8 - Total Weekly Mileage: 41

Coaching Points: Work on doing some balance exercises every day, just a few minutes of standing on one leg per day, throughout the day.

Good relaxed running form should be coming naturally.

Continue working on cadence by working your arm drive. Keep a close eye on your running stats and look to make progress each week.

Monday - 5 miles easy

Tuesday

- 1 mile easy
- 2 sets x 3 reps x 800m repeats
- 200m slow active recovery between reps
- 2 minutes static recovery between sets
- Target each rep: 3:25-3:30/rep
- 1 mile easy

Wednesday - Rest day

Thursday - 6 miles steady

Friday - Rest day
Saturday - 7 miles easy
Sunday - 18 miles LSD

3:45 Plan
Week 9 - **Total Weekly Mileage: 42**
Coaching Points: Work on doing some balance exercises every day, just a few minutes of standing on one leg per day, throughout the day.

Good relaxed running form should be coming naturally.

Continue working on cadence and working on your arm drive. Look at your stats from your running sessions and if you still need work, we can try another method. I'm not one to listen to music when I run, but it is a good way to work on cadence. So if you are not making progress, try running with music, but ensure your playlist has songs with 180 beats per minute. There are plenty of playlists out there that are designed for this.

Monday - 4 miles easy
Tuesday - 8 miles hilly run
Wednesday - No running
Thursday - 6 mile progression up to 7:40/mile for last mile
Friday - Rest day

Saturday - 9 miles steady
Sunday - 15 miles LSD

3:45 Plan
Week 10 - Total Weekly Mileage: 45
Coaching Points: Work on doing some balance exercises every day, just a few minutes of standing on one leg per day, throughout the day.

Good relaxed running form should be coming naturally.

Continue working on cadence and working on your arm drive and possibly listening to 180 beats per minute playlists.

Monday - 3 miles easy
Tuesday - 6 miles @ 8:15/mile pace
Wednesday

- 1 mile easy
- 4 x 1200m repeats
- 200m slow active recovery between reps
- Target each rep: 5:30-5:35 / rep
- 1 mile easy

Thursday - 6 miles steady
Friday - Rest day

Saturday

- 1 mile easy
- 3 @ 8:15/mile
- 1 mile easy

Sunday - 20 miles LSD

3:45 Plan

Week 11 - **Total Weekly Mileage: 34**

Coaching Points: Work on doing some balance exercises every day, just a few minutes of standing on one leg per day, throughout the day.

Good relaxed running form should be coming naturally.

Continue working on cadence and working on your arm drive and possibly listening to 180 beats per minute playlists.

Monday - 5 miles easy

Tuesday

- 1 mile easy
- 5 miles @ 8:00/mile pace
- 1 mile easy

Wednesday - Rest day
Thursday - 5 miles steady
Friday - No running
Saturday - 4 miles steady
Sunday - 13 miles LSD

3:45 Plan
Week 12 - Total Weekly Mileage: 39
Coaching Points: Work on doing some balance exercises every day, just a few minutes of standing on one leg per day, throughout the day.

Good relaxed running form should be coming naturally.

Continue working on cadence and working on your arm drive and possibly listening to 180 beats per minute playlists.

Monday - 5 miles easy
Tuesday - Rest day
Wednesday

- 1 mile easy
- 4 x 1 mile repeats @ 7:30/mile pace
- 2 minutes slow jog recovery between reps
- 1 mile easy

Thursday - 5 miles easy
Friday - No running
Saturday - 5 miles steady
Sunday - 18 miles LSD

3:45 Plan
Week 13 - Total Weekly Mileage: 45
Coaching Points: Work on doing some balance exercises every day, just a few minutes of standing on one leg per day, throughout the day.

Good relaxed running form should be coming naturally. Cadence should be better than when you started.

Now we will start focussing on mental strength. As we approach the final Race Phase of the plan, it is time to really focus on positive self-talk, visualization, and affirmations. Reinforce all the work you've done but ensuring no negative thoughts or doubts slip into your head. Zero negativity!

Monday - 5 miles easy
Tuesday

- 1 mile easy
- 4 miles @ 7:50/mile
- 1 mile easy

Wednesday - Rest day
Thursday - 7 miles steady
Friday - No running
Saturday - 5 miles steady
Sunday

- 12 miles LSD
- + 10 miles @ 8:30/mile
- Complete this as a single run

3:45 Plan
Week 14 - Total Weekly Mileage: 32
Coaching Points: Work on doing some balance exercises every day, just a few minutes of standing on one leg per day, throughout the day.

Good relaxed running form should be coming naturally. Cadence should be better than when you started.

Stay positive, practice daily positive self-talk, visualization and affirmations. Self-belief is key. You have earned your upcoming personal record.

Monday - 3 miles easy
Tuesday

- 1 mile easy
- 5 x 1k reps
- 200m active slow jog recovery
- Target rep each: 4:35-4:45
- 1 mile easy

Wednesday - 3 miles easy
Thursday - Rest day
Friday

- 1 mile easy
- 4 miles @ 7:50/mile
- 1 mile easy

Saturday - No running
Sunday

- 7 miles @ 8:30/mile
- + 8 miles LSD
- Complete this as a single run

3:45 Plan
Week 15 - **Total Weekly Mileage: 30**
Coaching Points: Work on doing some balance exercises
Coaching Points: Work on doing some balance exercises

every day, just a few minutes of standing on one leg per day, throughout the day.

Good relaxed running form should be coming naturally. Cadence should be better than when you started.

Stay positive, practice daily positive self-talk, visualization and affirmations. Self-belief is key. You have earned your upcoming personal record.

Monday - 5 miles easy
Tuesday

- 1 mile easy
- 2 miles @ 7:40/mile
- 1 mile easy

Wednesday - Rest day
Thursday - 5 miles easy
Friday - Rest day
Saturday

- 1 mile easy
- 1 mile @ 7:30/mile
- 1 mile easy

Sunday - 13 miles LSD

3:45 Plan

Week 16 - **Total Weekly Mileage: 34.2**

Coaching Points: You have arrived at race week. Everything will come together this week. Trust your training. Trust yourself and your coach. You have put in all the work. Now all you need to do is stay positive, keep the positive self-talk working in your favor and execute your race plan.

Monday - Rest day

Tuesday

- 1 mile easy
- 1 mile @ 7:30/mile
- 1 mile easy

Wednesday - Rest day
Thursday - 3 miles easy
Friday - Rest day
Saturday - 2 miles very easy
Sunday - RACE DAY (26.2 miles)

Target Pace: 8:30/mile

SUB 3:30 PLAN - MEDIUM MILEAGE PLAN

3:30 Plan

Week 1 - Total Weekly Mileage: 29

Coaching Points: Work on doing some balance exercises every day, just a few minutes of standing on one leg per day, throughout the day.

Focus on good running form, especially on the easy and steady runs. Running tall, chest forward with shoulders relaxed and down in your posture.

Monday - 5 miles easy
Tuesday - No running
Wednesday - 5 miles easy

Thursday - 6 miles easy
Friday - Rest day
Saturday - 3 miles steady
Sunday - 10 miles LSD

3:30 Plan

Week 2 - Total Weekly Mileage: 30

Coaching Points: Work on doing some balance exercises every day, just a few minutes of standing on one leg per day, throughout the day.

Focus on good running form, especially on the easy and steady runs. Running tall, chest forward with shoulders relaxed and down in your posture.

Monday - 5 miles easy
Tuesday

- 1 mile easy
- 2 sets of 6 x 60 second hill repeats. No recovery between reps and 90 seconds between sets
- 1 mile easy

Wednesday - No running
Thursday - 4 miles easy
Friday - Rest day

Saturday

- 1 mile easy
- 3 miles steady
- 1 mile easy

Sunday - 11 miles LSD

3:30 Plan
Week 3 - Total Weekly Mileage: 33
Coaching Points: Work on doing some balance exercises every day, just a few minutes of standing on one leg per day, throughout the day.

Focus on good running form, especially on the easy and steady runs. Running tall, chest forward with shoulders relaxed and down in your posture.

Monday - 5 miles easy
Tuesday - 6 mile hilly run
Wednesday - No running
Thursday - 5 miles easy
Friday - Rest day
Saturday

- 1 mile easy

- 3 miles steady
- 1 mile easy

Sunday - 12 miles LSD

3:30 Plan

Week 4 - Total Weekly Mileage: 37

Coaching Points: Work on doing some balance exercises every day, just a few minutes of standing on one leg per day, throughout the day.

Focus on good running form, especially on the easy and steady runs. Running tall, chest forward with shoulders relaxed and down in your posture.

Monday - 4 miles easy

Tuesday

- 1 mile easy
- 3 sets of 4 x 90 second hill repeats. No recovery between reps and 90 seconds between sets
- 2 miles easy

Wednesday - No running

Thursday

- 1 mile easy
- 4 miles @ 7:25/mile pace
- 1 mile easy

Friday - 3 miles easy

Saturday

- 1 mile easy
- 3 miles steady
- 2 miles easy

Sunday - 13 miles LSD

3:30 Plan

Week 5 - Total Weekly Mileage: 41

Coaching Points: Work on doing some balance exercises every day, just a few minutes of standing on one leg per day, throughout the day.

Focus on good running form, especially on the easy and steady runs. Running tall, chest forward with shoulders relaxed and down in your posture. With 4 weeks of good running form, good habits will start to be ingrained. Keep a good focus on these things.

Now is a good time to start looking at cadence. The technical running model calls for a cadence of at least 180 strides per minute. Look at your stats from your running sessions and if you are under this average on your runs, particularly your steady and faster runs, it is time to work on arm-drive. Your arm swing determines how fast your legs turnover. Start here by driving your arms faster and with purpose, this will increase your cadence naturally. Try to increase your cadence, even slightly each week, over the next weeks.

Monday - 5 miles easy
Tuesday - 6 miles steady
Wednesday - No running
Thursday

- 5 miles progression
- First mile at 8:30
- Last mile @ 7:00

Friday - 6 miles easy
Saturday - 4 miles @ 7:25/mile pace
Sunday - 15 miles LSD

3:30 Plan
Week 6 - **Total Weekly Mileage: 43**
Coaching Points: Work on doing some balance exercises

every day, just a few minutes of standing on one leg per day, throughout the day.

Good relaxed running form should be coming naturally.

Continue working on cadence by working your arm drive. Keep a close eye on your running stats and look to make progress each week.

Monday - 5 miles easy

Tuesday

- 1 mile easy
- 3 sets of 4 reps x 400m repeats
- 200m slow active recovery between reps
- 2 minutes between sets
- Target pace per rep: 90-95 seconds
- 1 mile easy

Wednesday - Rest day

Thursday - 7 miles easy

Friday

- 1 mile easy
- 3 miles @ 7:25/mile pace
- 1 mile easy

Saturday - 5 miles steady
Sunday - 16 miles LSD

3:30 Plan
Week 7 - Total Weekly Mileage: 38

Coaching Points: Work on doing some balance exercises every day, just a few minutes of standing on one leg per day, throughout the day.

Good relaxed running form should be coming naturally.

Continue working on cadence by working your arm drive. Keep a close eye on your running stats and look to make progress each week.

Monday - 4 miles easy
Tuesday

- 6 miles progression run
- First mile @ 8:20/mile pace
- Last mile @ 7:00/mile

Wednesday - No running
Thursday - 5 miles steady
Friday - Rest day
Saturday

- 1 mile easy
- 4 miles @ 7:20/mile pace
- 1 mile easy

Sunday - 17 miles LSD

3:30 Plan

Week 8 - Total Weekly Mileage: 40

Coaching Points: Work on doing some balance exercises every day, just a few minutes of standing on one leg per day, throughout the day.

Good relaxed running form should be coming naturally.

Continue working on cadence by working your arm drive. Keep a close eye on your running stats and look to make progress each week.

Monday - 4 miles easy

Tuesday

- 1 mile easy
- 2 sets x 3 reps x 800m repeats
- 200m slow active recovery between reps
- 2 minutes static recovery between sets
- Target each rep: 3:15-3:20/rep

- 1 mile easy

Wednesday - No running
Thursday - 6 miles steady
Friday - Rest day
Saturday - 7 miles steady
Sunday - 18 miles LSD

3:30 Plan

Week 9 - **Total Weekly Mileage: 45**

Coaching Points: Work on doing some balance exercises every day, just a few minutes of standing on one leg per day, throughout the day.

Good relaxed running form should be coming naturally.

Continue working on cadence and working on your arm drive. Look at your stats from your running sessions and if you still need work, we can try another method. I'm not one to listen to music when I run, but it is a good way to work on cadence. So if you are not making progress, try running with music, but ensure your playlist has songs with 180 beats per minute. There are plenty of playlists out there that are designed for this.

Monday - 4 miles easy

Tuesday - 8 miles hilly run
Wednesday - Rest day
Thursday - 6 mile progression up to 7:15/mile for last mile
Friday - 3 miles easy
Saturday - 9 miles steady
Sunday - 15 miles LSD

3:30 Plan
Week 10 - **Total Weekly Mileage: 49**
Coaching Points: Work on doing some balance exercises every day, just a few minutes of standing on one leg per day, throughout the day.

Good relaxed running form should be coming naturally.

Continue working on cadence and working on your arm drive and possibly listening to 180 beats per minute playlists.

Monday - 3 miles easy
Tuesday

- 1 mile easy
- 4 miles @ 7:45/mile pace
- 1 mile easy

Wednesday

- 1 mile easy
- 4 x 1200m repeats
- 200m slow active recovery between reps
- Target each rep: 4:55-5:05 / rep
- 1 mile easy

Thursday - 9 miles easy
Friday - Rest day
Saturday

- 1 mile easy
- 3 @ 7:20/mile
- 1 mile easy

Sunday - 20 miles LSD

3:30 Plan
Week 11 - Total Weekly Mileage: 38
Coaching Points: Work on doing some balance exercises every day, just a few minutes of standing on one leg per day, throughout the day.

Good relaxed running form should be coming naturally.

Continue working on cadence and working on your arm drive and possibly listening to 180 beats per minute playlists.

Monday - 4 miles easy
Tuesday

- 1 mile easy
- 5 miles @ 7:20/mile pace
- 1 mile easy

Wednesday - Rest day
Thursday - 5 miles steady
Friday - 5 miles easy
Saturday - 4 miles easy
Sunday - 13 miles LSD

3:30 Plan
Week 12 - Total Weekly Mileage: 42
Coaching Points: Work on doing some balance exercises every day, just a few minutes of standing on one leg per day, throughout the day.

Good relaxed running form should be coming naturally.

Continue working on cadence and working on your arm drive and possibly listening to 180 beats per minute playlists.

Monday - 4 miles easy
Tuesday

- 1 mile easy
- 5 x 1 mile repeats @ 6:55/mile pace
- 2 minutes slow jog recovery between reps
- 1 mile easy

Wednesday - Rest day
Thursday - 5 miles easy
Friday - 3 miles easy
Saturday - 5 miles steady
Sunday - 18 miles LSD

3:30 Plan
Week 13 - **Total Weekly Mileage: 51**
Coaching Points: Work on doing some balance exercises every day, just a few minutes of standing on one leg per day, throughout the day.

Good relaxed running form should be coming naturally. Cadence should be better than when you started.

Now we will start focussing on mental strength. As we approach the final Race Phase of the plan, it is time to really focus on positive self-talk, visualization, and affirmations. Reinforce all the work you've done but ensuring no negative thoughts or doubts slip into your head. Zero negativity!

Monday - 5 miles easy
Tuesday

- 1 mile easy
- 4 miles @ 7:15/mile
- 1 mile easy

Wednesday - Rest day
Thursday - 7 miles steady
Friday

- 1 mile easy
- 2 miles @ 7:15/mile pace
- 1 mile easy

Saturday - 5 miles easy
Sunday

- 12 miles LSD
- + 12 miles @ 8:00/mile
- Complete this as a single run

3:30 Plan
Week 14 - Total Weekly Mileage: 39
Coaching Points: Work on doing some balance exercises

every day, just a few minutes of standing on one leg per day, throughout the day.

Good relaxed running form should be coming naturally. Cadence should be better than when you started.

Stay positive, practice daily positive self-talk, visualization and affirmations. Self-belief is key. You have earned your upcoming personal record.

Monday - 3 miles easy
Tuesday

- 1 mile easy
- 2 sets of 4 reps x 1k repeats
- 200m active slow jog recovery
- Target rep each: 4:15-4:20
- 1 mile easy

Wednesday - 3 miles easy
Thursday - Rest day
Friday

- 1 mile easy
- 4 miles @ 7:15/mile
- 1 mile easy

Saturday - No running

Sunday

- 10 miles @ 7:45/mile pace
- + 10 miles LSD
- To be completed as a single run

3:30 Plan

Week 15 - Total Weekly Mileage: 30

Coaching Points: Work on doing some balance exercises every day, just a few minutes of standing on one leg per day, throughout the day.

Good relaxed running form should be coming naturally. Cadence should be better than when you started.

Stay positive, practice daily positive self-talk, visualization and affirmations. Self-belief is key. You have earned your upcoming personal record.

Monday - 5 miles easy

Tuesday

- 1 mile easy
- 2 miles @ 7:15/mile
- 1 mile easy

Wednesday - Rest day
Thursday - 5 miles easy
Friday - Rest day
Saturday

- 1 mile easy
- 1 mile @ 7:00/mile
- 1 mile easy

Sunday - 13 miles LSD

3:30 Plan
Week 16 - **Total Weekly Mileage: 34.2**
Coaching Points: You have arrived at race week. Everything will come together this week. Trust your training. Trust yourself and your coach. You have put in all the work. Now all you need to do is stay positive, keep the positive self-talk working in your favor and execute your race plan.

Monday - Rest day
Tuesday

- 1 mile easy
- 1 mile @ 7:00/mile
- 1 mile easy

Wednesday - Rest day

Thursday - 3 miles easy

Friday - Rest day

Saturday - 2 miles very easy

Sunday - RACE DAY (26.2 miles)

Target Pace: 7:55/mile

SUB 3:15 PLAN - MEDIUM MILEAGE PLAN

3:15 Plan

Week 1 - Total Weekly Mileage: 29

Coaching Points: Work on doing some balance exercises every day, just a few minutes of standing on one leg per day, throughout the day.

Focus on good running form, especially on the easy and steady runs. Running tall, chest forward with shoulders relaxed and down in your posture.

Monday - 5 miles easy
Tuesday - No running
Wednesday - 5 miles steady
Thursday - 6 miles easy

Friday - Rest day
Saturday - 3 miles steady
Sunday - 10 miles LSD

3:15 Plan

Week 2 - **Total Weekly Mileage: 30**

Coaching Points: Work on doing some balance exercises every day, just a few minutes of standing on one leg per day, throughout the day.

Focus on good running form, especially on the easy and steady runs. Running tall, chest forward with shoulders relaxed and down in your posture.

Monday - 5 miles easy
Tuesday

- 1 mile easy
- 2 sets of 8 x 60 second hill repeats. No recovery between reps and 90 seconds between sets
- 1 mile easy

Wednesday - No running
Thursday - 4 miles easy
Friday - Rest day
Saturday

- 1 mile easy
- 3 miles steady
- 1 mile easy

Sunday - 11 miles LSD

3:15 Plan
Week 3 - **Total Weekly Mileage: 35**
Coaching Points: Work on doing some balance exercises every day, just a few minutes of standing on one leg per day, throughout the day.

Focus on good running form, especially on the easy and steady runs. Running tall, chest forward with shoulders relaxed and down in your posture.

Monday - 4 miles easy
Tuesday - 6 mile hilly run
Wednesday - No running
Thursday - 5 miles easy
Friday - 3 miles easy
Saturday

- 1 mile easy
- 3 miles steady
- 1 mile easy

Sunday - 12 miles LSD

3:15 Plan
Week 4 - **Total Weekly Mileage: 37**
Coaching Points: Work on doing some balance exercises every day, just a few minutes of standing on one leg per day, throughout the day.

Focus on good running form, especially on the easy and steady runs. Running tall, chest forward with shoulders relaxed and down in your posture.

Monday - 4 miles easy
Tuesday

- 1 mile easy
- 3 sets of 5 x 90 second hill repeats. No recovery between reps and 90 seconds between sets
- 2 miles easy

Wednesday - No running
Thursday

- 1 mile easy
- 4 miles @ 7:00/mile pace
- 1 mile easy

Friday - 3 miles easy
Saturday

- 1 mile easy
- 4 miles steady
- 1 mile easy

Sunday - 13 miles LSD

3:15 Plan
Week 5 - Total Weekly Mileage: 42
Coaching Points: Work on doing some balance exercises every day, just a few minutes of standing on one leg per day, throughout the day.

Focus on good running form, especially on the easy and steady runs. Running tall, chest forward with shoulders relaxed and down in your posture. With 4 weeks of good running form, good habits will start to be ingrained. Keep a good focus on these things.

Now is a good time to start looking at cadence. The technical running model calls for a cadence of at least 180 strides per minute. Look at your stats from your running sessions and if you are under this average on your runs, particularly your steady and faster runs, it is time to work on arm-drive. Your arm swing determines how fast your legs turnover. Start here by driving your arms faster and with purpose, this will increase your cadence naturally. Try to increase your cadence, even slightly each week, over the next weeks.

Monday - 5 miles easy
Tuesday - 8 miles steady
Wednesday - No running
Thursday

- 5 miles progression
- First mile at 8:20
- Last mile @ 6:50

Friday - 5 miles easy
Saturday - 4 miles @ 7:00/mile pace
Sunday - 15 miles LSD

3:15 Plan
Week 6 - Total Weekly Mileage: 43
Coaching Points: Work on doing some balance exercises every day, just a few minutes of standing on one leg per day, throughout the day.

Good relaxed running form should be coming naturally.

Continue working on cadence by working your arm drive. Keep a close eye on your running stats and look to make progress each week.

Monday - 5 miles easy
Tuesday

- 1 mile easy
- 3 sets of 4 reps x 400m repeats
- 200m slow active recovery between reps
- 2 minutes between sets
- Target pace per rep: 85-90 seconds
- 1 mile easy

Wednesday - Rest day
Thursday - 7 miles easy
Friday

- 1 mile easy
- 3 miles @ 7:00/mile pace
- 1 mile easy

Saturday - 5 miles steady
Sunday - 16 miles LSD

3:15 Plan

Week 7 - Total Weekly Mileage: 40

Coaching Points: Work on doing some balance exercises every day, just a few minutes of standing on one leg per day, throughout the day.

Good relaxed running form should be coming naturally.

Continue working on cadence by working your arm drive. Keep a close eye on your running stats and look to make progress each week.

Monday - 5 miles easy
Tuesday

- 6 miles progression run
- First mile @ 8:00/mile pace
- Last mile @ 6:50/mile

Wednesday - No running
Thursday - 6 miles steady
Friday - Rest day
Saturday

- 1 mile easy
- 4 miles @ 7:00/mile pace
- 1 mile easy

Sunday - 17 miles LSD

3:15 Plan
Week 8 - Total Weekly Mileage: 43
Coaching Points: Work on doing some balance exercises every day, just a few minutes of standing on one leg per day, throughout the day.

Good relaxed running form should be coming naturally.

Continue working on cadence by working your arm drive. Keep a close eye on your running stats and look to make progress each week.

Monday - 5 miles easy
Tuesday

- 1 mile easy
- 2 sets x 3 reps x 800m repeats
- 200m slow active recovery between reps
- 2 minutes static recovery between sets
- Target each rep: 3:00-3:05/rep
- 1 mile easy

Wednesday - No running
Thursday - 6 miles steady

Friday - Rest day

Saturday

- 1 mile easy
- 7 miles steady
- 1 mile easy

Sunday - 18 miles LSD

3:15 Plan

Week 9 - Total Weekly Mileage: 45

Coaching Points: Work on doing some balance exercises every day, just a few minutes of standing on one leg per day, throughout the day.

Good relaxed running form should be coming naturally.

Continue working on cadence and working on your arm drive. Look at your stats from your running sessions and if you still need work, we can try another method. I'm not one to listen to music when I run, but it is a good way to work on cadence. So if you are not making progress, try running with music, but ensure your playlist has songs with 180 beats per minute. There are plenty of playlists out there that are designed for this.

Monday - 4 miles easy
Tuesday - 8 miles hilly run
Wednesday - Rest day
Thursday - 6 mile progression up to 6:50/mile for last mile
Friday - 3 miles easy
Saturday - 9 miles steady
Sunday - 15 miles LSD

3:15 Plan
Week 10 - Total Weekly Mileage: 54
Coaching Points: Work on doing some balance exercises every day, just a few minutes of standing on one leg per day, throughout the day.

Good relaxed running form should be coming naturally.

Continue working on cadence and working on your arm drive and possibly listening to 180 beats per minute playlists.

Monday - 3 miles easy
Tuesday

- 1 mile easy
- 6 miles @ 7:30/mile pace
- 1 mile easy

Wednesday

- 1 mile easy
- 4 x 1200m repeats
- 200m slow active recovery between reps
- Target each rep: 4:35-4:45 / rep
- 1 mile easy

Thursday - 9 miles easy

Friday - 4 miles easy

Saturday

- 1 mile easy
- 3 @ 6:55/mile
- 1 mile easy

Sunday - 20 miles LSD

3:15 Plan

Week 11 - Total Weekly Mileage: 38

Coaching Points: Work on doing some balance exercises every day, just a few minutes of standing on one leg per day, throughout the day.

Good relaxed running form should be coming naturally.

Continue working on cadence and working on your arm drive and possibly listening to 180 beats per minute playlists.

Monday - 4 miles easy
Tuesday

- 1 mile easy
- 5 miles @ 6:55/mile pace
- 1 mile easy

Wednesday - Rest day
Thursday - 5 miles steady
Friday - 5 miles easy
Saturday - 4 miles easy
Sunday - 13 miles LSD

3:15 Plan
Week 12 - Total Weekly Mileage: 42
Coaching Points: Work on doing some balance exercises every day, just a few minutes of standing on one leg per day, throughout the day.

Good relaxed running form should be coming naturally.

Continue working on cadence and working on your arm drive and possibly listening to 180 beats per minute playlists.

Monday - 4 miles easy

Tuesday

- 1 mile easy
- 5 x 1 mile repeats @ 6:30/mile pace
- 2 minutes slow jog recovery between reps
- 1 mile easy

Wednesday - Rest day
Thursday - 5 miles easy
Friday - 3 miles easy
Saturday - 5 miles steady
Sunday - 18 miles LSD

3:15 Plan

Week 13 - Total Weekly Mileage: 52

Coaching Points: Work on doing some balance exercises every day, just a few minutes of standing on one leg per day, throughout the day.

Good relaxed running form should be coming naturally. Cadence should be better than when you started.

Now we will start focussing on mental strength. As we approach the final Race Phase of the plan, it is time to really focus on positive self-talk, visualization, and affirmations.

Reinforce all the work you've done but ensuring no negative thoughts or doubts slip into your head. Zero negativity!

Monday - 5 miles easy

Tuesday

- 1 mile easy
- 4 miles @ 6:55/mile
- 1 mile easy

Wednesday - Rest day

Thursday - 7 miles steady

Friday

- 1 mile easy
- 3 miles @ 6:55/mile pace
- 1 mile easy

Saturday - 5 Miles easy

Sunday

- 12 miles @ 7:20/mile
- + 12 miles LSD
- Complete this as a single run

3:15 Plan

Week 14 - Total Weekly Mileage: 39

Coaching Points: Work on doing some balance exercises every day, just a few minutes of standing on one leg per day, throughout the day.

Good relaxed running form should be coming naturally. Cadence should be better than when you started.

Stay positive, practice daily positive self-talk, visualization and affirmations. Self-belief is key. You have earned your upcoming personal record.

Monday - 3 miles easy
Tuesday

- 1 mile easy
- 2 sets x 4 reps x 1k repeats
- 200m active slow jog recovery
- Target rep each: 4:00-4:05
- 1 mile easy

Wednesday - 3 miles easy
Thursday - Rest day
Friday

- 1 mile easy

- 4 miles @ 6:50/mile
- 1 mile easy

Saturday - No running

Sunday

- 10 miles @ 7:15/mile pace
- + 10 miles LSD
- To be completed as a single run

3:15 Plan

Week 15 - Total Weekly Mileage: 32

Coaching Points: Work on doing some balance exercises every day, just a few minutes of standing on one leg per day, throughout the day.

Good relaxed running form should be coming naturally. Cadence should be better than when you started.

Stay positive, practice daily positive self-talk, visualization and affirmations. Self-belief is key. You have earned your upcoming personal record.

Monday - 5 miles easy

Tuesday

- 1 mile easy
- 2 miles @ 6:50/mile
- 1 mile easy

Wednesday - Rest day
Thursday - 5 miles easy
Friday - Rest day
Saturday

- 1 mile easy
- 3 mile @ 6:50/mile
- 1 mile easy

Sunday - 13 miles LSD

3:15 Plan

Week 16 - **Total Weekly Mileage: 34.2**

Coaching Points: You have arrived at race week. Everything will come together this week. Trust your training. Trust yourself and your coach. You have put in all the work. Now all you need to do is stay positive, keep the positive self-talk working in your favor and execute your race plan.

Monday - Rest day
Tuesday

- 1 mile easy
- 1 mile @ 6:45/mile
- 1 mile easy

Wednesday - Rest day
Thursday - 3 miles easy
Friday - Rest day
Saturday - 2 miles very easy
Sunday - RACE DAY (26.2 miles)

Target Pace: 7:20/mile

SUB 3:00 PLAN - HIGH MILEAGE PLAN

3:00 Plan

Week 1 - Total Weekly Mileage: 33

Coaching Points: Work on doing some balance exercises every day, just a few minutes of standing on one leg per day, throughout the day.

Focus on good running form, especially on the easy and steady runs. Running tall, chest forward with shoulders relaxed and down in your posture.

Monday - 6 miles steady
Tuesday - No running
Wednesday - 5 miles steady
Thursday - 6 miles easy

Friday - Rest day

Saturday

- 1 mile easy
- 3 miles steady
- 2 miles easy

Sunday - 10 miles LSD

3:00 Plan

Week 2 - Total Weekly Mileage: 40

Coaching Points: Work on doing some balance exercises every day, just a few minutes of standing on one leg per day, throughout the day.

Focus on good running form, especially on the easy and steady runs. Running tall, chest forward with shoulders relaxed and down in your posture.

Monday - No running

Tuesday

- 2 miles easy
- 3 sets of 6 x 60 second hill repeats. No recovery between reps and 90 seconds between sets
- 3 miles easy

Wednesday - 6 miles easy
Thursday - 7 miles easy
Friday - Rest day
Saturday

- 1 mile easy
- 3 miles steady
- 2 miles easy

Sunday - 13 miles LSD

3:00 Plan
Week 3 - Total Weekly Mileage: 44
Coaching Points: Work on doing some balance exercises every day, just a few minutes of standing on one leg per day, throughout the day.

Focus on good running form, especially on the easy and steady runs. Running tall, chest forward with shoulders relaxed and down in your posture.

Monday - No running
Tuesday

- 2 miles easy

- 3 sets of 5 x 90 second hill repeats. No recovery between reps and 90 seconds between sets
- 1 mile easy

Wednesday - 6 miles easy
Thursday - 9 miles easy
Friday - Rest day
Saturday

- 2 miles easy
- 3 miles steady
- 3 miles easy

Sunday - 14 miles LSD

3:00 Plan
Week 4 - **Total Weekly Mileage: 50**
Coaching Points: Work on doing some balance exercises every day, just a few minutes of standing on one leg per day, throughout the day.

Focus on good running form, especially on the easy and steady runs. Running tall, chest forward with shoulders relaxed and down in your posture.

Monday - No running

Tuesday

- 1 mile easy
- 6 miles steady
- 1 mile easy

Wednesday - 6 miles easy
Thursday - 8 miles easy
Friday - 8 miles @ 7:20/mile pace
Saturday - 4 miles steady
Sunday - 16 miles LSD

3:00 Plan
Week 5 - Total Weekly Mileage: 53
Coaching Points: Work on doing some balance exercises every day, just a few minutes of standing on one leg per day, throughout the day.

Focus on good running form, especially on the easy and steady runs. Running tall, chest forward with shoulders relaxed and down in your posture. With 4 weeks of good running form, good habits will start to be ingrained. Keep a good focus on these things.

Now is a good time to start looking at cadence. The technical running model calls for a cadence of at least 180 strides per minute. Look at your stats from your running sessions and if you are under this average on your runs, particularly your steady and faster runs, it is time to work on arm-drive. Your arm swing determines how fast your legs turnover. Start here by driving your arms faster and with purpose, this will increase your cadence naturally. Try to increase your cadence, even slightly each week, over the next weeks.

Monday - 4 miles easy
Tuesday - 6 miles hilly run
Wednesday - 10 miles easy
Thursday

- 7 mile progression run
- First mile @ 8:00/mile pace
- Last mile @ 6:30/mile pace

Friday - Rest day
Saturday

- 2 miles easy
- 4 miles @ 6:45/mile pace
- 2 miles easy

Sunday - 18 miles LSD

3:00 Plan

Week 6 - Total Weekly Mileage: 56

Coaching Points: Work on doing some balance exercises every day, just a few minutes of standing on one leg per day, throughout the day.

Good relaxed running form should be coming naturally.

Continue working on cadence by working your arm drive. Keep a close eye on your running stats and look to make progress each week.

Monday - 4 miles easy

Tuesday

- 1 mile easy
- 8 x 1k reps
- 200m active slow jog recovery
- Target rep each: 3:45-3:50/rep
- 1 mile easy

Wednesday - 6 miles easy

Thursday

- 5 miles @ 7:40/mile in the morning
- 5 miles @ 6:40/mile in the evening

Friday - Rest day
Saturday

- 2 miles easy
- 5 miles @ 6:45/mile pace
- 2 miles easy

Sunday - 20 miles LSD

3:00 Plan
Week 7 - **Total Weekly Mileage: 56**
Coaching Points: Work on doing some balance exercises every day, just a few minutes of standing on one leg per day, throughout the day.

Good relaxed running form should be coming naturally.

Continue working on cadence by working your arm drive. Keep a close eye on your running stats and look to make progress each week.

Monday - 3 miles easy
Tuesday - 8 miles steady
Wednesday - 12 miles easy
Thursday - Rest day
Friday

- 1 mile easy
- 3 miles @ 6:35/mile pace
- 1 mile easy

Saturday - 5 miles steady
Sunday - 23 miles LSD

3:00 Plan
Week 8 - Total Weekly Mileage: 40
Coaching Points: Work on doing some balance exercises every day, just a few minutes of standing on one leg per day, throughout the day.

Good relaxed running form should be coming naturally.

Continue working on cadence by working your arm drive. Keep a close eye on your running stats and look to make progress each week.

Monday - 4 miles easy
Tuesday - No running
Wednesday - 8 miles hilly
Thursday - 5 miles steady
Friday - Rest day
Saturday - 3 miles steady
Sunday - 20 miles LSD

3:00 Plan
Week 9 - **Total Weekly Mileage: 60**

Coaching Points: Work on doing some balance exercises every day, just a few minutes of standing on one leg per day, throughout the day.

Good relaxed running form should be coming naturally.

Continue working on cadence and working on your arm drive. Look at your stats from your running sessions and if you still need work, we can try another method. I'm not one to listen to music when I run, but it is a good way to work on cadence. So if you are not making progress, try running with music, but ensure your playlist has songs with 180 beats per minute. There are plenty of playlists out there that are designed for this.

Monday - 5 miles easy

Tuesday

- 1 miles easy
- 2 sets of 4 reps x 1200m reps
- 200m slow active recovery between reps
- 90 seconds static recovery between sets
- Target rep each: 4:15-4:20
- 1 miles easy

Wednesday - 13 miles easy
Thursday - 6 mile progression up to 6:25/mile for last mile
Friday - 4 miles easy
Saturday - 10 miles @ 6:50/mile pace
Sunday - 14 miles LSD

3:00 Plan

Week 10 - Total Weekly Mileage: 55

Coaching Points: Work on doing some balance exercises every day, just a few minutes of standing on one leg per day, throughout the day.

Good relaxed running form should be coming naturally.

Continue working on cadence and working on your arm drive and possibly listening to 180 beats per minute playlists.

Monday - No running

Tuesday

- 1 mile easy
- 4 miles @ 6:40/mile pace
- 1 mile easy

Wednesday - 6 miles easy
Thursday - 14 miles steady

Friday - Rest
Saturday

- 3 miles easy
- 5 @ 6:30/mile
- 3 mile easy

Sunday - 18 miles LSD

3:00 Plan
Week 11 - **Total Weekly Mileage: 64**
Coaching Points: Work on doing some balance exercises every day, just a few minutes of standing on one leg per day, throughout the day.

Good relaxed running form should be coming naturally. Cadence should be better than where it was.

Let's do some work on stride length. Over the next four weeks make an effort to increase your stride length, just slightly. You do not want to reach with your leading leg, instead, open your stride behind you. To do this try to get your trailing leg to come up just about hitting your backside on each stride. Nothing drastic, this isn't the time to change your stride altogether, but a slight improvement can mean a lot over 26.2 miles.

Monday - 5 miles easy

Tuesday

- 1 mile easy warm up
- 2 sets x 3 reps x 1 mile repeats
- 200m active recovery between reps
- 2 minutes static recovery between sets
- Target rep each: 5:50-5:55
- 1 mile easy

Wednesday - 3 miles steady

Thursday - 10 mile progression up top 6:30 for last mile

Friday

- 4 miles easy in the morning
- 4 miles easy in the evening

Saturday - 7 miles steady

Sunday - 23 miles LSD

3:00 Plan
Week 12 - Total Weekly Mileage: 45

Coaching Points: Work on doing some balance exercises every day, just a few minutes of standing on one leg per day, throughout the day.

Good relaxed running form should be coming naturally. Cadence should be better than when you started.

Continue working on your stride length, looking for small improvements over these next three weeks.

Monday - 3 miles easy
Tuesday - 3 miles easy
Wednesday - 13 miles steady
Thursday - 5 miles easy
Friday - Rest day
Saturday

- 1 mile easy
- 4 miles @ 6:30/mile
- 1 mile easy

Sunday - 15 miles LSD

3:00 Plan
Week 13 - **Total Weekly Mileage: 60**
Coaching Points: Work on doing some balance exercises every day, just a few minutes of standing on one leg per day, throughout the day.

Good relaxed running form should be coming naturally.

Cadence should be better than when you started.

Continue working on your stride length, looking for small improvements over these next two weeks.

Monday - No running

Tuesday

- 1 mile easy
- 4 x 2k reps
- 60 seconds static recovery between reps
- Target rep each: 7:29-7:39
- 1 mile easy

Wednesday - 10 miles easy

Thursday

- 6 miles steady in the morning
- 6 miles easy in the evening

Friday - Rest day

Saturday - 9 miles steady

Sunday

- 11 miles @ 6:45/mile
- + 11 miles LSD

- Complete this as a single run

3:00 Plan
Week 14 - Total Weekly Mileage: 69

Coaching Points: Work on doing some balance exercises every day, just a few minutes of standing on one leg per day, throughout the day.

Good relaxed running form should be coming naturally. Cadence should be better than when you started.

Continue working on stride length and fine tuning anything else that needs work.

Monday - 3 miles easy
Tuesday - 8 miles easy
Wednesday - 20 miles LSD
Thursday - 3 miles easy
Friday - 5 miles easy
Saturday

- 1 mile easy
- 4 miles steady
- 1 mile easy

Sunday

- 12 miles @ 6:45/mile pace
- + 12 miles LSD
- To be completed as a single run

3:00 Plan

Week 15 - Total Weekly Mileage: 58

Coaching Points: Work on doing some balance exercises every day, just a few minutes of standing on one leg per day, throughout the day.

Good relaxed running form should be coming naturally.
Cadence should be better than when you started.
Stride length should be better than when you started.

Now we will start focussing on mental strength. In this final Race Phase of the plan, it is time to really focus on positive self-talk, visualization, and affirmations. Reinforce all the work you've done but ensuring no negative thoughts or doubts slip into your head. Zero negativity!

Monday - 3 miles easy
Tuesday - 22 miles LSD
Wednesday - 12 miles easy
Thursday - Rest day
Friday - 5 miles steady
Saturday - 3 miles steady

Sunday - 13 miles LSD

3:00 Plan

Week 16 - Total Weekly Mileage: 34.2

Coaching Points: You have arrived at race week. Everything will come together this week. Trust your training. Trust yourself and your coach. You have put in all the work. Now all you need to do is stay positive, keep the positive self-talk working in your favor and execute your race plan.

Monday - Rest day

Tuesday

- 1 mile easy
- 1 mile @ 6:30/mile
- 1 mile easy

Wednesday - Rest day
Thursday - 3 miles easy
Friday - Rest day
Saturday - 2 miles very easy
Sunday - RACE DAY (26.2 miles)

Target Pace: 6:45/mile

SUB 2:45 PLAN - HIGH MILEAGE PLAN

2:45 Plan

Week 1 - Total Weekly Mileage: 33

Coaching Points: Work on doing some balance exercises every day, just a few minutes of standing on one leg per day, throughout the day.

Focus on good running form, especially on the easy and steady runs. Running tall, chest forward with shoulders relaxed and down in your posture.

Monday - 6 miles steady
Tuesday - No running
Wednesday - 5 miles steady
Thursday - 6 miles easy

Friday - Rest day

Saturday

- 1 mile easy
- 3 miles steady
- 2 miles easy

Sunday - 10 miles LSD

2:45 Plan
Week 2 - Total Weekly Mileage: 40

Coaching Points: Work on doing some balance exercises every day, just a few minutes of standing on one leg per day, throughout the day.

Focus on good running form, especially on the easy and steady runs. Running tall, chest forward with shoulders relaxed and down in your posture.

Monday - No running

Tuesday

- 2 miles easy
- 3 sets of 6 x 60 second hill repeats. No recovery between reps and 90 seconds between sets
- 3 miles easy

Wednesday - 6 miles easy
Thursday - 7 miles easy
Friday - Rest day
Saturday

- 1 mile easy
- 3 miles steady
- 2 miles easy

Sunday - 13 miles LSD

2:45 Plan
Week 3 - Total Weekly Mileage: 44
Coaching Points: Work on doing some balance exercises every day, just a few minutes of standing on one leg per day, throughout the day.

Focus on good running form, especially on the easy and steady runs. Running tall, chest forward with shoulders relaxed and down in your posture.

Monday - No running
Tuesday

- 2 miles easy

- 3 sets of 5 x 90 second hill repeats. No recovery between reps and 90 seconds between sets
- 1 miles easy

Wednesday - 6 miles easy
Thursday - 9 miles easy
Friday - Rest day
Saturday

- 2 miles easy
- 3 miles steady
- 3 miles easy

Sunday - 14 miles LSD

2:45 Plan
Week 4 - Total Weekly Mileage: 50
Coaching Points: Work on doing some balance exercises every day, just a few minutes of standing on one leg per day, throughout the day.

Focus on good running form, especially on the easy and steady runs. Running tall, chest forward with shoulders relaxed and down in your posture.

Monday - No running

Tuesday

- 1 mile easy
- 6 miles steady
- 1 mile easy

Wednesday - 6 miles easy
Thursday - 8 miles easy
Friday - 8 miles @ 6:50/mile pace
Saturday - 4 miles steady
Sunday - 16 miles LSD

2:45 Plan
Week 5 - Total Weekly Mileage: 53

Coaching Points: Work on doing some balance exercises every day, just a few minutes of standing on one leg per day, throughout the day.

Focus on good running form, especially on the easy and steady runs. Running tall, chest forward with shoulders relaxed and down in your posture. With 4 weeks of good running form, good habits will start to be ingrained. Keep a good focus on these things.

Now is a good time to start looking at cadence. The technical running model calls for a cadence of at least 180 strides per minute. Look at your stats from your running sessions and if you are under this average on your runs, particularly your steady and faster runs, it is time to work on arm-drive. Your arm swing determines how fast your legs turnover. Start here by driving your arms faster and with purpose, this will increase your cadence naturally. Try to increase your cadence, even slightly each week, over the next weeks.

Monday - 4 miles easy
Tuesday - 6 miles hilly run
Wednesday - 10 miles easy
Thursday

- 7 mile progression run
- First mile @ 7:30/mile pace
- Last mile at 5:50/mile pace

Friday - Rest day
Saturday

- 2 miles easy
- 4 miles @ 6:10/mile pace
- 2 miles easy

Sunday - 18 miles LSD

2:45 Plan

Week 6 - Total Weekly Mileage: 56

Coaching Points: Work on doing some balance exercises every day, just a few minutes of standing on one leg per day, throughout the day.

Good relaxed running form should be coming naturally.

Continue working on cadence by working your arm drive. Keep a close eye on your running stats and look to make progress each week.

Monday - 4 miles easy

Tuesday

- 1 mile easy
- 8 x 1k reps
- 200m active slow jog recovery
- Target rep each: 3:15-3:22/rep
- 1 mile easy

Wednesday - 6 miles easy

Thursday

- 5 miles @ 7:00/mile in the morning
- 5 miles @ 6:00/mile in the evening

Friday - Rest day

Saturday

- 2 miles easy
- 5 miles @ 6:30/mile pace
- 2 miles easy

Sunday - 20 miles LSD

2:45 Plan

Week 7 - **Total Weekly Mileage: 57**

Coaching Points: Work on doing some balance exercises every day, just a few minutes of standing on one leg per day, throughout the day.

Good relaxed running form should be coming naturally.

Continue working on cadence by working your arm drive. Keep a close eye on your running stats and look to make progress each week.

Monday - 3 miles easy
Tuesday - 8 miles steady
Wednesday - 12 miles easy
Thursday - Rest day
Friday

- 1 mile easy
- 3 miles @ 5:50/mile pace
- 1 mile easy

Saturday - 5 miles steady
Sunday - 24 miles LSD

2:45 Plan
Week 8 - Total Weekly Mileage: 40
Coaching Points: Work on doing some balance exercises every day, just a few minutes of standing on one leg per day, throughout the day.

Good relaxed running form should be coming naturally.

Continue working on cadence by working your arm drive. Keep a close eye on your running stats and look to make progress each week.

Monday - 4 miles easy
Tuesday - 6 miles hilly
Wednesday - No running
Thursday - 7 miles steady
Friday - Rest day
Saturday - 3 miles steady
Sunday - 20 miles LSD

2:45 Plan

Week 9 - Total Weekly Mileage: 60

Coaching Points: Work on doing some balance exercises every day, just a few minutes of standing on one leg per day, throughout the day.

Good relaxed running form should be coming naturally.

Continue working on cadence and working on your arm drive. Look at your stats from your running sessions and if you still need work, we can try another method. I'm not one to listen to music when I run, but it is a good way to work on cadence. So if you are not making progress, try running with music, but ensure your playlist has songs with 180 beats per minute. There are plenty of playlists out there that are designed for this.

Monday - 3 miles easy

Tuesday

- 1 mile easy
- 2 sets x 4 reps x 1200m reps
- 200m slow active recovery between repeats
- 90 seconds static recovery between sets
- Target rep each: 3:45-3:55
- 1 mile easy

Wednesday - 10 miles easy
Thursday - 6 mile progression up to 5:45/mile for last mile
Friday - 9 miles easy
Saturday - 10 miles @ 6:15/mile pace
Sunday - 14 miles LSD

2:45 Plan
Week 10 - Total Weekly Mileage: 60

Coaching Points: Work on doing some balance exercises every day, just a few minutes of standing on one leg per day, throughout the day.

Good relaxed running form should be coming naturally.

Continue working on cadence and working on your arm drive and possibly listening to 180 beats per minute playlists.

Monday - No running
Tuesday

- 2 mile easy
- 4 miles @ 6:10/mile pace
- 2 mile easy

Wednesday - 8 miles easy
Thursday - 14 miles steady

Friday - Rest day
Saturday

- 3 miles easy
- 5 @ 6:00/mile
- 3 mile easy

Sunday - 19 miles LSD

2:45 Plan
Week 11 - Total Weekly Mileage: 70
Coaching Points: Work on doing some balance exercises every day, just a few minutes of standing on one leg per day, throughout the day.

Good relaxed running form should be coming naturally. Cadence should be better than where it was.

Let's do some work on stride length. Over the next four weeks make an effort to increase your stride length, just slightly. You do not want to reach with your leading leg, instead, open your stride behind you. To do this try to get your trailing leg to come up just about hitting your backside on each stride. Nothing drastic, this isn't the time to change your stride altogether, but a slight improvement can mean a lot over 26.2 miles.

Monday - 5 miles easy
Tuesday

- 2 miles easy
- 2 sets x 3 reps x 1 mile repeats
- 200m active recovery between reps
- 2 minutes static recovery between sets
- Target rep each: 5:25-5:30
- 2 miles easy

Wednesday - 3 miles steady
Thursday - 10 mile progression up to 5:45 for last mile
Friday

- 7 miles easy in the morning
- 5 miles easy in the evening

Saturday - 7 miles steady
Sunday - 23 miles LSD

2:45 Plan
Week 12 - Total Weekly Mileage: 44
Coaching Points: Work on doing some balance exercises every day, just a few minutes of standing on one leg per day, throughout the day.

Good relaxed running form should be coming naturally. Cadence should be better than when you started.

Continue working on your stride length, looking for small improvements over these next three weeks.

Monday - 3 miles easy
Tuesday - Rest day
Wednesday - 10 miles steady
Thursday - 8 miles easy
Friday - Rest day
Saturday

- 2 miles easy
- 4 miles @ 5:50/mile
- 2 miles easy

Sunday - 15 miles LSD

2:45 Plan
Week 13 - **Total Weekly Mileage: 62**
Coaching Points: Work on doing some balance exercises every day, just a few minutes of standing on one leg per day, throughout the day.

Good relaxed running form should be coming naturally.

Cadence should be better than when you started.

Continue working on your stride length, looking for small improvements over these next two weeks.

Monday - No running
Tuesday

- 1 mile easy
- 4 x 2k reps
- 60 seconds static recovery between reps
- Target rep each: 7:05-7:15
- 1 mile easy

Wednesday - 12 miles easy
Thursday

- 6 miles steady in the morning
- 6 miles easy in the evening

Friday - Rest day
Saturday - 9 miles steady
Sunday

- 11 miles @ 6:10/mile
- + 11 miles LSD

- Complete this as a single run

2:45 Plan
Week 14 - Total Weekly Mileage: 67
Coaching Points: Work on doing some balance exercises every day, just a few minutes of standing on one leg per day, throughout the day.

Good relaxed running form should be coming naturally. Cadence should be better than when you started.

Continue working on stride length and fine tuning anything else that needs work.

Monday - 3 miles easy
Tuesday - 8 miles easy
Wednesday - 20 miles easy
Thursday - Rest day
Friday - 6 miles easy
Saturday

- 1 mile easy
- 4 miles @ 6:40/mile
- 1 mile easy

Sunday

- 12 miles @ 6:15/mile pace
- + 12 miles LSD
- To be completed as a single run

2:45 Plan

Week 15 - Total Weekly Mileage: 64

Coaching Points: Work on doing some balance exercises every day, just a few minutes of standing on one leg per day, throughout the day.

Good relaxed running form should be coming naturally.
Cadence should be better than when you started.
Stride length should be better than when you started.

Now we will start focussing on mental strength. In this final Race Phase of the plan, it is time to really focus on positive self-talk, visualization, and affirmations. Reinforce all the work you've done but ensuring no negative thoughts or doubts slip into your head. Zero negativity!

Monday - 3 miles easy
Tuesday - 22 miles LSD
Wednesday - 20 miles LSD
Thursday - 3 miles easy
Friday - Rest day
Saturday - 3 miles steady

Sunday - 13 miles LSD

2:45 Plan
Week 16 - Total Weekly Mileage: 34.2

Coaching Points: You have arrived at race week. Everything will come together this week. Trust your training. Trust yourself and your coach. You have put in all the work. Now all you need to do is stay positive, keep the positive self-talk working in your favor and execute your race plan.

Monday - Rest day
Tuesday

- 1 mile easy
- 1 mile @ 6:00/mile
- 1 mile easy

Wednesday - Rest day
Thursday - 3 miles easy
Friday - Rest day
Saturday - 2 miles very easy
Sunday - RACE DAY (26.2 miles)

Target Pace: 6:15/mile

You've done it!

If you enjoyed *Marathon Training Strategies: A Comprehensive Guide to Running Your Best Marathon - Including Plans, Advice and Goal-Hitting Tips*, **please leave a positive review of this book on Amazon or wherever you purchased it**. It is so important to coaches and authors who are producing quality work for distribution. It is a great way for this book to be put in front of more people.

I've enjoyed working with you and please look for more of my books and training programs by browsing Amazon. You will find more books for the beginners and intermediate runners in your life. These offer easy to follow programs for hitting distance and speed goals. For now, bask in the greatness of what you just achieved. I am proud of you and you should be proud of yourself!

Browse all on my books Amazon author page.

If you are interested in learning more about the my life experience or need some additional inspiration, my memoir *A Heart for Running: How Running Saved My Life* is available on Amazon.

I have created an online community of runners of all abilities called Achieve Running Club. This includes a blog where I share content from a coaching perspective or opinions from a runner or coaching perspective. It can be found at achieverc.com. Additionally, there is a Strava Club, where the community acts as a support network for each other to share our running training and experiences.

There are also all of the usual social media suspects, each of which is listed below.

I would very much like to hear from you with feedback. I am extremely interested in your results from your target marathon. Please provide some feedback on one of the following links:

Blog - https://achieverc.com
Facebook - https://www.facebook.com/groups/achieverc
Instagram - https://instagram.com/achieverunningclub
Twitter - https://x.com/achieverunners
YouTube - https://youtube.com/@achieverunningclub

I also have a blog dedicated to my personal running and life experiences at A Heart for Running. I take great interest in all runners and would love to hear from you, so please do reach out in one form or another.

ALSO BY JOHN MCDONNELL

A Heart for Running: How Running Saved My Life

Running for Beginners: The Easiest Guide to Running Your First 5K In Only 6 Weeks

Step Up to 10k: Improve Your 5k Time and Train for a 10k

www.ingramcontent.com/pod-product-compliance
Lightning Source LLC
Chambersburg PA
CBHW071232080526
44587CB00013BA/1578